Folk
Fest

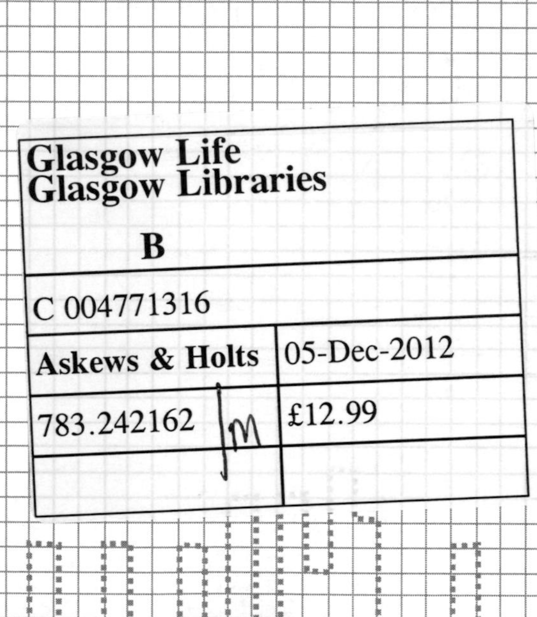

First published by Faber Music Ltd in 2006
3 Queen Square, London WC1N 3AU

Arranged by Frank Moon & Dave Weston
Engraved by Bassline
Compiled by Lucy Holliday
Edited by Lucy Holliday & Olly Weeks

Designed by Lydia Merrills-Ashcroft & Dominic Brookman
Sewn by Lydia with thanks to Sally Andrew

Printed in England by Caligraving Ltd

ISBN 0-571-52674-8

To buy Faber Music publications or to find out about the full range of titles available,
please contact your local music retailer or Faber Music sales enquiries:

Faber Music Ltd, Burnt Mill, Elizabeth Way, Harlow, CM20 2HX England
Tel: +44(0)1279 82 89 82 Fax: +44(0)1279 82 89 83
sales@fabermusic.com fabermusic.com

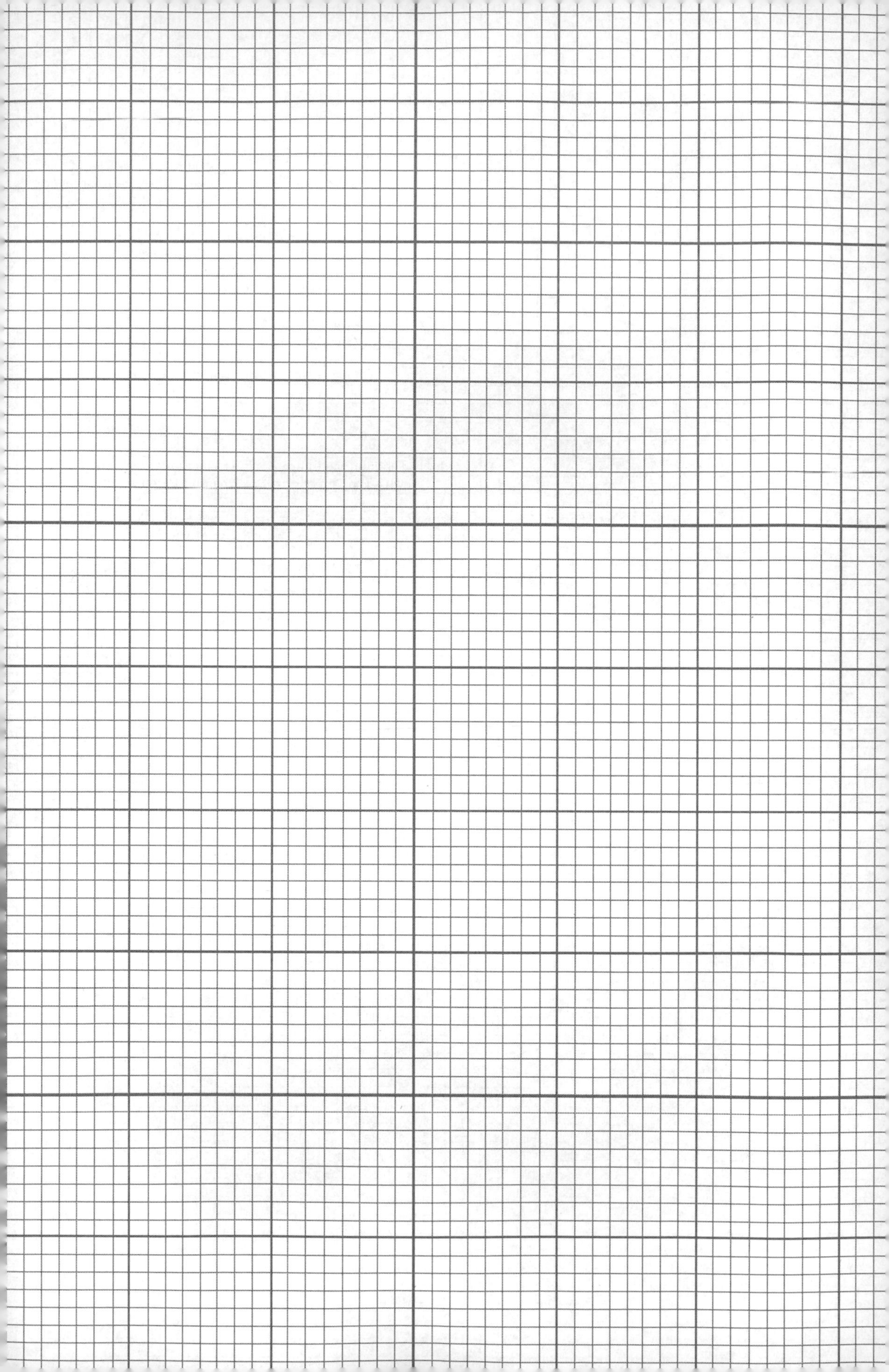

ALBION HEART

Words and Music by Julie Matthews and Christine While

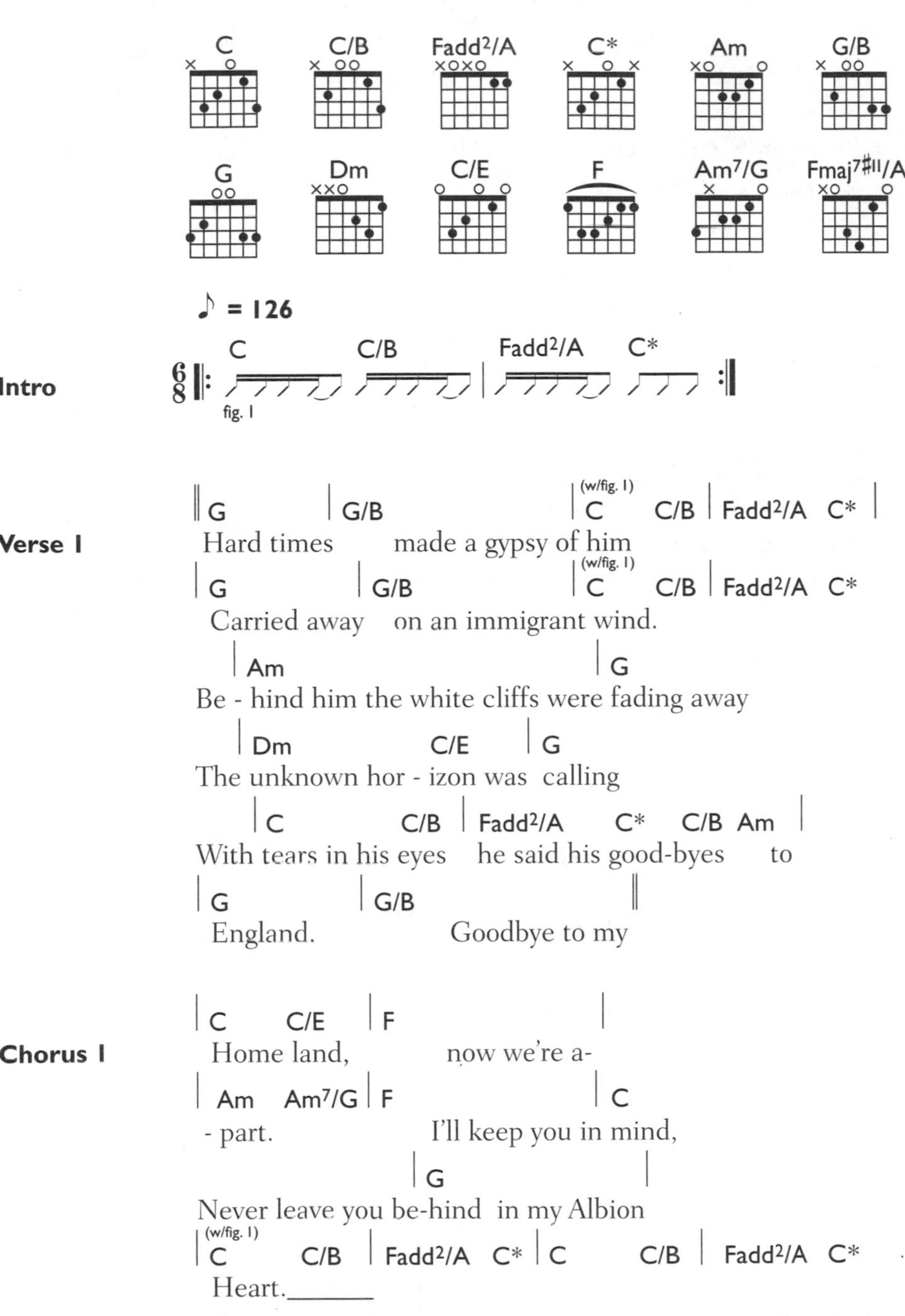
C
C/B
Fadd2/A
C*
Am
G/B
G
Dm
C/E
F
Am7/G
Fmaj7#11/A
♪ = 126
Intro
C C/B Fadd2/A C*
fig. 1
Verse 1
G G/B (w/fig. 1) C C/B Fadd2/A C*
Hard times made a gypsy of him
G G/B (w/fig. 1) C C/B Fadd2/A C*
Carried away on an immigrant wind.
Am G
Be - hind him the white cliffs were fading away
Dm C/E G
The unknown hor - izon was calling
C C/B Fadd2/A C* C/B Am
With tears in his eyes he said his good-byes to
G G/B
England. Goodbye to my
Chorus 1
C C/E F
Home land, now we're a-
Am Am7/G F C
- part. I'll keep you in mind,
G
Never leave you be-hind in my Albion
(w/fig. 1) C C/B Fadd2/A C* C C/B Fadd2/A C*
Heart.

Verse 2

```
  ║G          |G/B              |C (w/fig. 1)  C/B |Fadd2/A  C*
Oh she was born     of higher de - gree,_____
  |G          |G/B              |C (w/fig. 1)  C/B |Fadd2/A  C*
And their love,        they shared secretly._____
  |Am                     |G
In separate circles con - demned by his class
  |Dm               C/E   |G          |
He left for Am - erica's   shore
|C           C/B          |Fadd2/A      C*  C/B  Am  |
Vowing to come back a gentleman one   day to
|G            |G/B                 ║
 England.          Goodbye to my
```

Chorus 2

```
|C      C/E    |F                   |
 Home land,          now we're a-
| Am   Am7/G |F                 |C
- part.                I'll keep you in mind,
                          |G               |
Never leave you be-hind in my Albion
|C (w/fig. 1)  C/B  |Fadd2/A  C* ║
 Heart._____
```

Instrumental

```
║: Am                |Fmaj#11/A         :║ x3

║: C (w/fig. 1)   C/B    |Fadd2/A    C*    :║
```

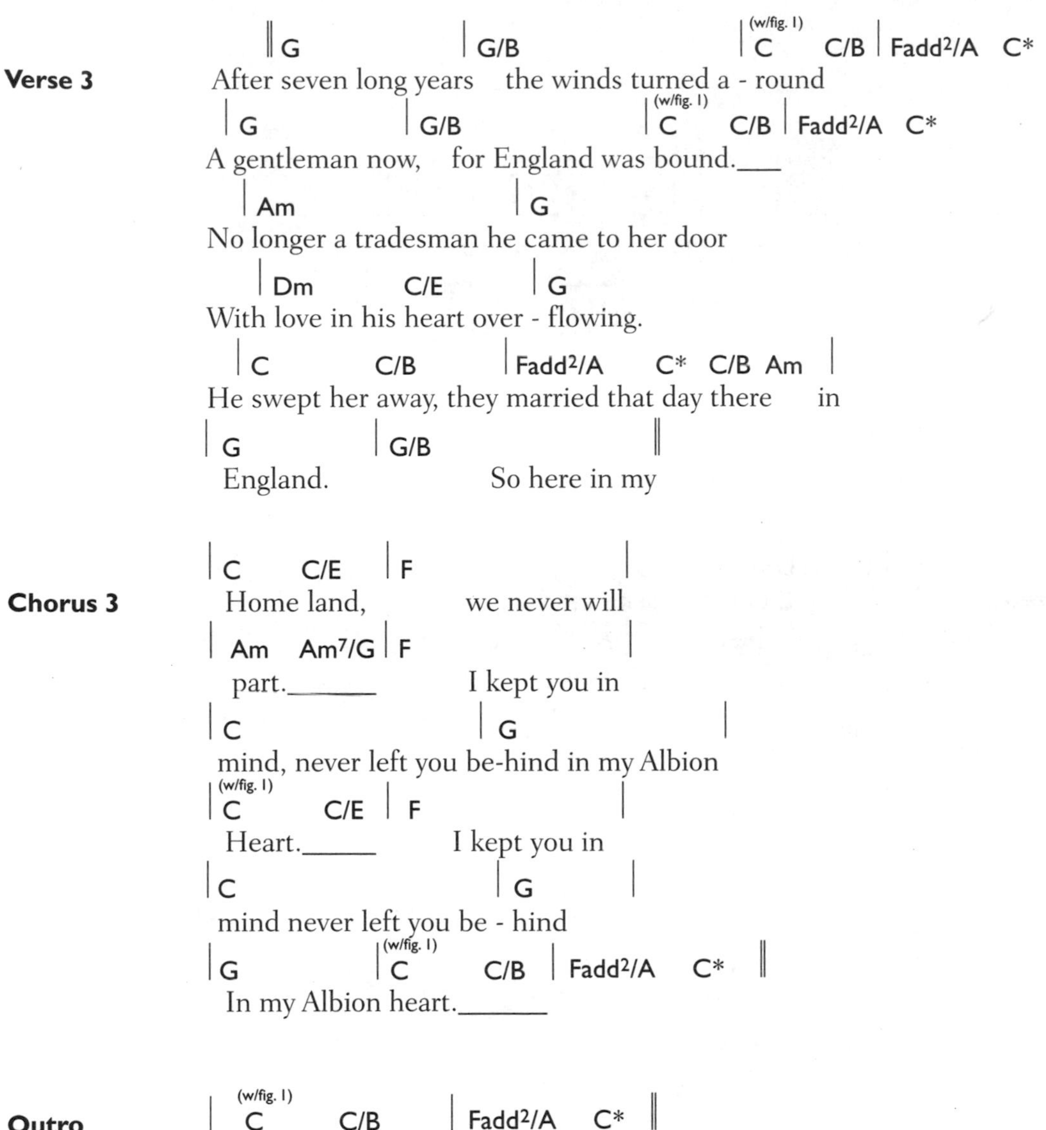
Verse 3
G G/B (w/fig. 1) C C/B Fadd2/A C*
After seven long years the winds turned a - round
G G/B (w/fig. 1) C C/B Fadd2/A C*
A gentleman now, for England was bound.
Am G
No longer a tradesman he came to her door
Dm C/E G
With love in his heart over - flowing.
C C/B Fadd2/A C* C/B Am
He swept her away, they married that day there in
G G/B
England. So here in my
Chorus 3
C C/E F
Home land, we never will
Am Am7/G F
part. I kept you in
C G
mind, never left you be-hind in my Albion
(w/fig. 1) C C/E F
Heart. I kept you in
C G
mind never left you be - hind
G (w/fig. 1) C C/B Fadd2/A C*
In my Albion heart.
Outro
(w/fig. 1) C C/B Fadd2/A C*

ANNIE'S SONG

Words and Music by John Denver

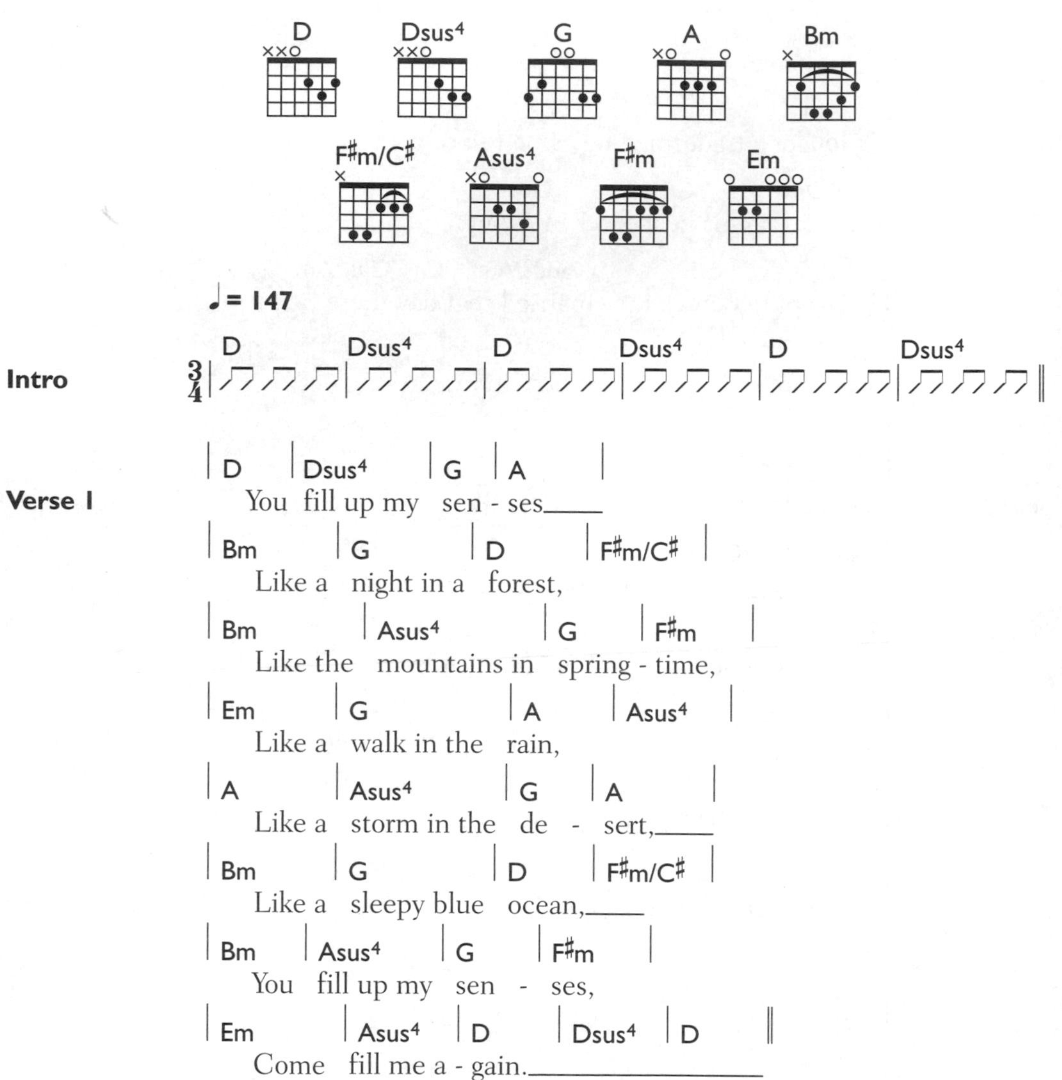
D
Dsus4
G
A
Bm
F#m/C#
Asus4
F#m
Em
♩= 147
Intro
D Dsus4 D Dsus4 D Dsus4
Verse 1
D Dsus4 G A
You fill up my sen - ses
Bm G D F#m/C#
Like a night in a forest,
Bm Asus4 G F#m
Like the mountains in spring - time,
Em G A Asus4
Like a walk in the rain,
A Asus4 G A
Like a storm in the de - sert,
Bm G D F#m/C#
Like a sleepy blue ocean,
Bm Asus4 G F#m
You fill up my sen - ses,
Em Asus4 D Dsus4 D
Come fill me a - gain.

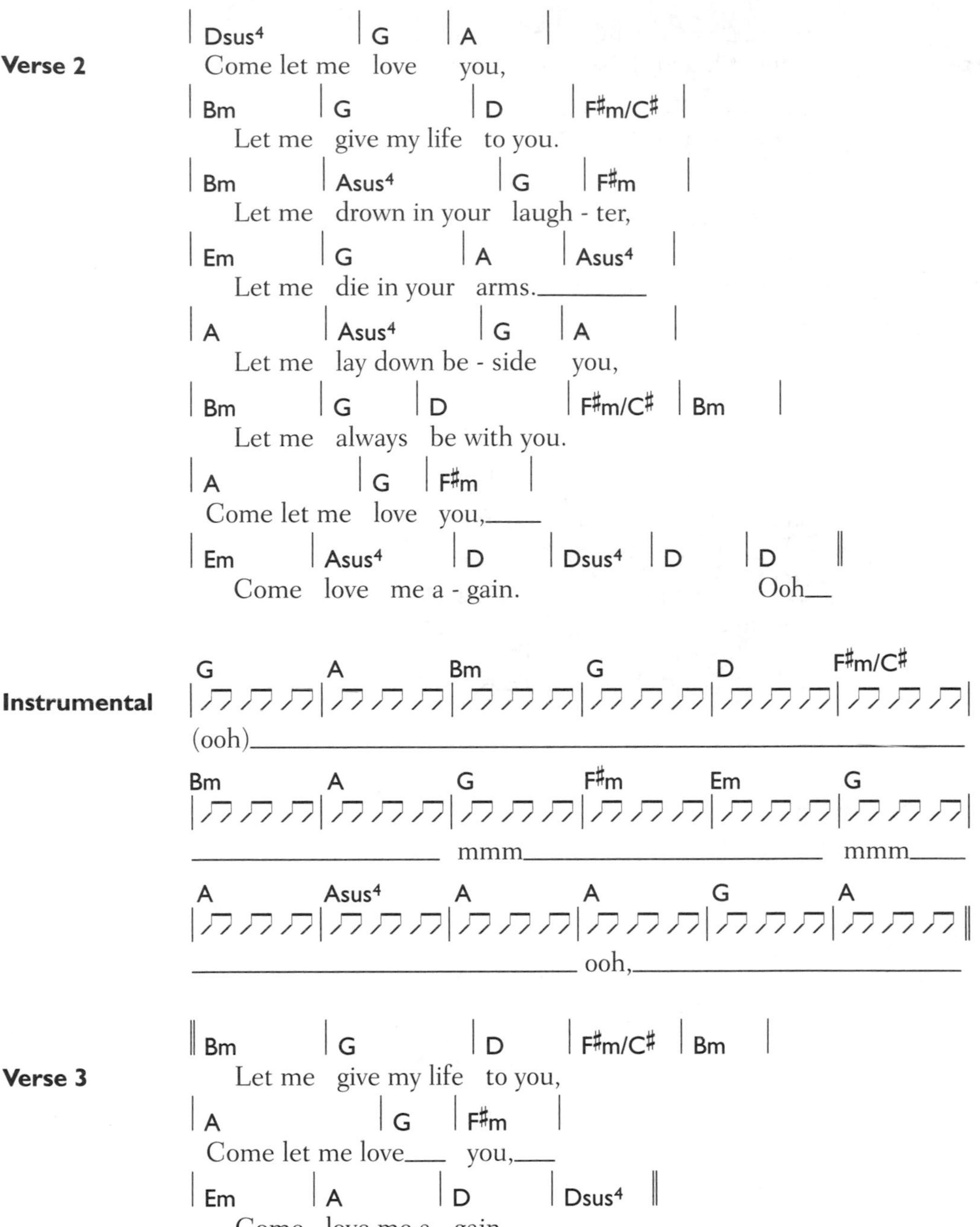

Verse 2
Dsus4 | G | A
Come let me love you,
Bm | G | D | F#m/C#
Let me give my life to you.
Bm | Asus4 | G | F#m
Let me drown in your laugh - ter,
Em | G | A | Asus4
Let me die in your arms.
A | Asus4 | G | A
Let me lay down be - side you,
Bm | G | D | F#m/C# | Bm
Let me always be with you.
A | G | F#m
Come let me love you,
Em | Asus4 | D | Dsus4 | D | D
Come love me a - gain. Ooh
Instrumental
G A Bm G D F#m/C#
(ooh)
Bm A G F#m Em G
mmm mmm
A Asus4 A A G A
ooh,
Verse 3
Bm | G | D | F#m/C# | Bm
Let me give my life to you,
A | G | F#m
Come let me love you,
Em | A | D | Dsus4
Come love me a - gain.

Verse 4

```
‖ D      | Dsus4      | G   | A        |
  You fill up my  sen - ses____
| Bm        | G          | D        | F#m/C# |
   Like a  night in a  forest,
| Bm           | Asus4          | G     | F#m    |
   Like the  mountains in  spring - time,
| Em         | G           | A      | Asus4  |
   Like a  walk in the   rain,________
| A          | Asus4        | G    | A       |
   Like a  storm in the  de  -  sert,___
slower                      a tempo
| Bm(fermata) | N.C.        | D     | F#m/C#  |
   Like a  sleepy blue  ocean,
| Bm    | A          | G     | F#m     |
   You  fill up my  sen  -  ses,
| Em         | Asus4  | D       | Dsus4  |
   Come  fill me a - gain.________
                          rit.
| D      | Dsus4  | D     | Dsus4  | D(fermata) ‖
________________________________
```

ANOTHER QUIET NIGHT IN ENGLAND

Words and Music by John Jones and Ian Telfer

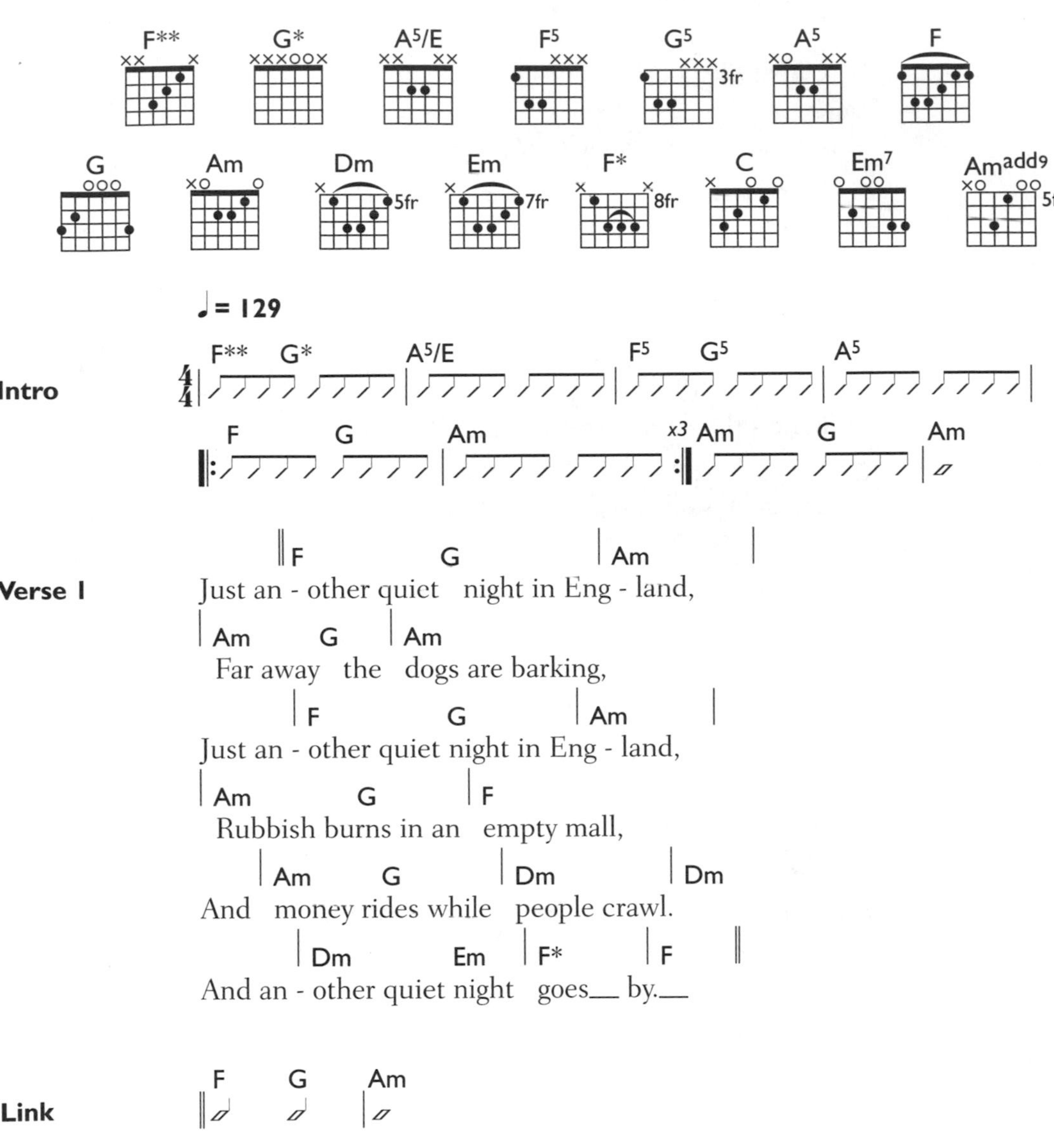
F** G* A5/E F5 G5 A5 F
3fr
G Am Dm Em F* C Em7 Amadd9
5fr 7fr 8fr 5fr
♩= 129
Intro
F** G* A5/E F5 G5 A5
F G Am x3 Am G Am
Verse 1
F G Am
Just an - other quiet night in Eng - land,
Am G Am
Far away the dogs are barking,
F G Am
Just an - other quiet night in Eng - land,
Am G F
Rubbish burns in an empty mall,
Am G Dm Dm
And money rides while people crawl.
Dm Em F* F
And an - other quiet night goes__ by.__
Link
F G Am

Verse 2

‖ F G | Am |
Just an - other quiet night in Eng - land,
| Am G | Am
Sleeping in some frozen doorway,
| F G | Am |
An - other quiet night in Eng - land,
| Am G | F
Every - where the game's the same,
| Am G | Dm | Dm
It's private wealth and pub - lic shame
| Dm Em | F* | F ‖
And an - other quiet night goes__ by.__

Chorus 1

‖ F C | F
Where is the pit and the mill?__
C | F G | Am |
Where is the skill and the strength of their hands?
| F C | F
Gone with the smoke and the heat,__
C | F *rit.* G | *a tempo* Am | Am ‖
The noise of the beat of the heart of the land.______

Violin solo 1

‖ F G Am | F Em7 Am |
| F G Am | Am G F |
| Am G Dm | Dm | Dm Em | F* F G |

Verse 3

‖ Am G | Am | Am G | Am
Just an - other quiet night in England, mmmm________
| Am G | Am
Just an - other quiet night in England,
| Am G | F
They turn away if you let it out,
| Am G | Dm | Dm
They think you're mad if you scream and shout, scream and shout,
| Dm Em | F* | F ‖
And an - other quiet night goes______ by.

Chorus 2

```
| F              C             | F
  Where is the pit and the mill?__
   C                 | F           G                | Am        |
Where is the skill   and the strength of their   hands?
| F                    C               | F
  Gone with the smoke and the heat,__
                                    rit.              a tempo
     C               | F            G               | Am       | Am      ||
The noise of the   beat of the heart of the   land.______ oh.__
```

Violin solo 2

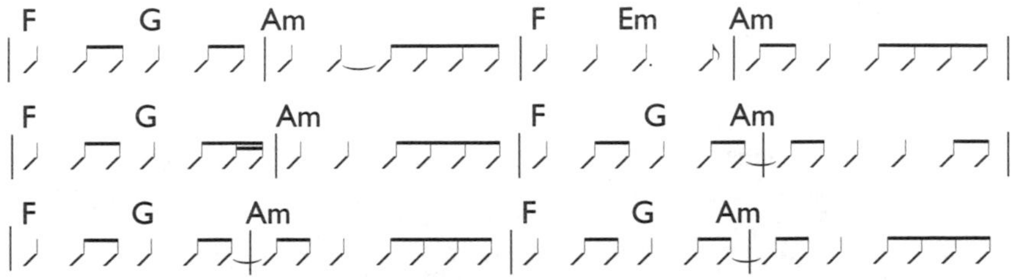

```
| F      G        Am                  | F      Em       Am               |
| F      G        Am                  | F      G        Am               |
| F      G        Am                  | F      G        Am
```

Outro

```
                                                  rit.
          | F         | G       | Am          | F        | G        | Amadd9 (fermata) ||
Just an - other quiet__ night__ in England.__
```

AT SEVENTEEN

Words and Music by Janis Ian

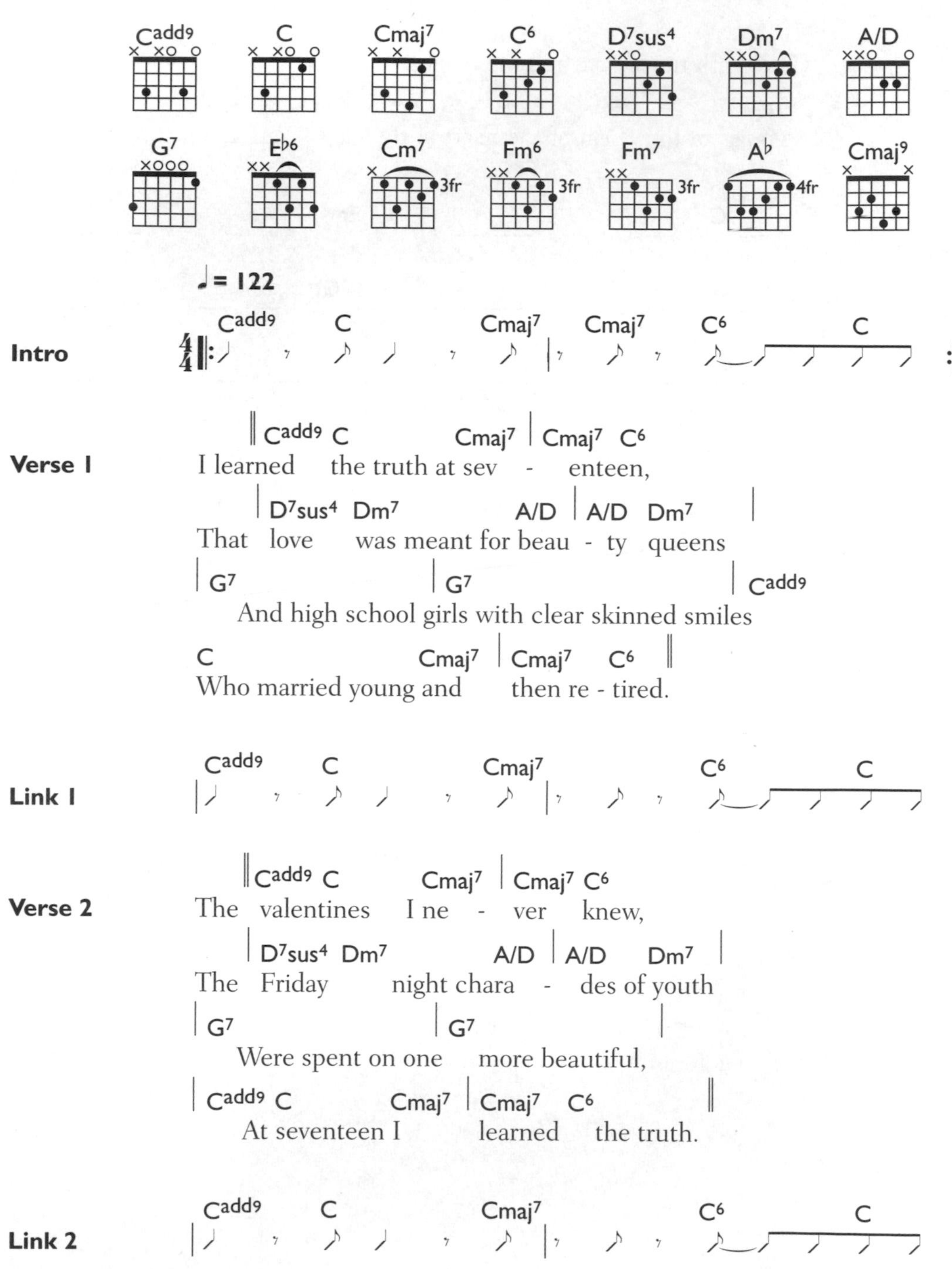
Cadd9
C
Cmaj7
C6
D7sus4
Dm7
A/D
G7
Eb6
Cm7
3fr
Fm6
3fr
Fm7
3fr
Ab
4fr
Cmaj9
♩= 122
Intro
Cadd9 C Cmaj7 Cmaj7 C6 C
Verse 1
Cadd9 C Cmaj7 Cmaj7 C6
I learned the truth at sev - enteen,
D7sus4 Dm7 A/D A/D Dm7
That love was meant for beau - ty queens
G7 G7 Cadd9
And high school girls with clear skinned smiles
C Cmaj7 Cmaj7 C6
Who married young and then re - tired.
Link 1
Cadd9 C Cmaj7 C6 C
Verse 2
Cadd9 C Cmaj7 Cmaj7 C6
The valentines I ne - ver knew,
D7sus4 Dm7 A/D A/D Dm7
The Friday night chara - des of youth
G7 G7
Were spent on one more beautiful,
Cadd9 C Cmaj7 Cmaj7 C6
At seventeen I learned the truth.
Link 2
Cadd9 C Cmaj7 C6 C

Chorus 1

‖ E♭6 | E♭6 |
And those of us with ra - vaged faces,
| Dm7 | G7 |
Lacking in the so - cial graces,
| Cm7 Fm6 | Fm6 Fm7
Desperately re - main - ed at home,
| Cm7 Fm6 | Fm6
In - venting lovers on____ the phone.
| A♭ G7 | G7 |
Who called to say – "Come dance with me,"
| Cm7 Fm6 | Fm6 Fm7 |
And murmured vague obscenities,
| Dm7 | Dm7 | G7 | G7
It isn't all it seems at seventeen.

Verse 3

‖ Cadd9 C Cmaj7 | Cmaj7 C6
A brown eyed girl in hand____ me downs,
| D7sus4 Dm7 A/D | A/D Dm7 |
Whose name I never could pronounce,
| G7 | G7 |
Said "Pity please the ones who serve,
| Cadd9 C Cmaj7 | Cmaj7 C6 ‖
They only get what they deserve."

Link 3

Cadd9 C Cmaj7 C6 C

Verse 4

‖ Cadd9 C Cmaj7 | Cmaj7 C6 |
And the rich relationed home - town queen
| D7sus4 Dm7 A/D | A/D Dm7
Mar - ries into what she needs
| G7 | G7
With a gua - rantee of com - pany
| Cadd9 C Cmaj7 | Cmaj7 C6 ‖
And ha - ven for the elder - ly.

Link 4

Cadd9 C Cmaj7 C6 C

Chorus 2

|| E♭6 | E♭6 |
Remem - ber those who win___ the game,
| Dm7 | G7
Lose the love they sought to gain,
| Cm7 | Fm6 Fm7 | Cm7 | Fm6 Fm7
In debentures of qua - li - ty and dubious in - te - gri - ty,
| A♭ | G7
Their small-town eyes will gape at you
| Cm7 | Fm6 Fm7 |
In dull surprise when payment due
| Dm7 | Dm7 | G7 | G7 ||
Exceeds accounts received at seventeen.

Instrumental

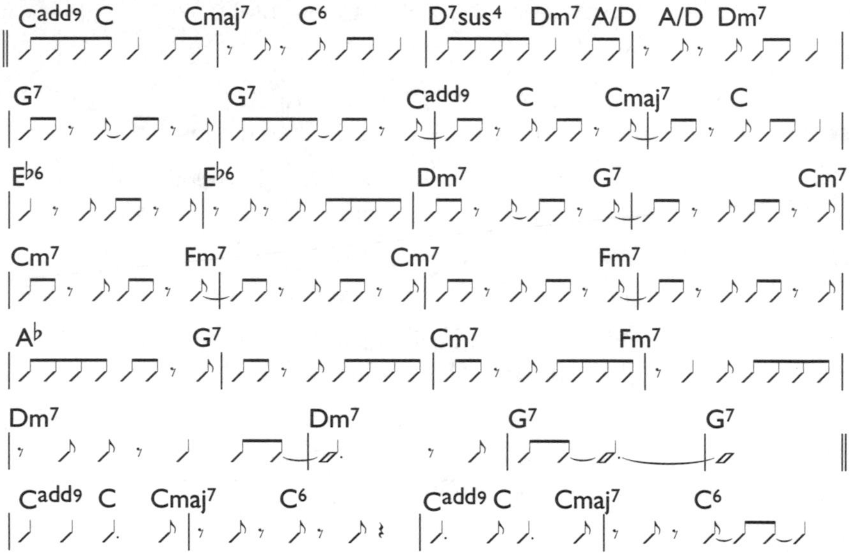

	Cadd9 C Cmaj7	C6	D7sus4 Dm7 A/D	A/D Dm7
G7	G7	Cadd9 C	Cmaj7 C
E♭6	E♭6	Dm7 G7	Cm7
Cm7 Fm7	Cm7 Fm7
A♭	G7	Cm7	Fm7
Dm7	Dm7	G7	G7	
Cadd9 C Cmaj7	C6	Cadd9 C Cmaj7	C6

Verse 5

|| Cadd9 C Cmaj7 | Cmaj7 C6
To those of us who knew the pain
| D7sus4 Dm7 A/D | A/D Dm7 |
Of va - lentines that never came,
| G7 | G7 |
And those whose names were never called
| Cadd9 C Cmaj7 | Cmaj7 C6 ||
When choosing sides for basketball.

Link 5

| Cadd9 C Cmaj7 | C6 C |

Verse 6

‖ Cadd9 C Cmaj7 | Cmaj7 C6 |
It was long a - go and far______ away

| D7sus4 Dm7 A/D | A/D Dm7 |
The world was younger than today

| G7 | G7 |
When dreams were all they gave for free

| Cadd9 C Cmaj7 | Cmaj7 C6 | Cadd9 C Cmaj7 | Cmaj7
To ugly duck - ling girls__ like___ me.

Chorus 3

C6 ‖ E♭6 | E♭6
We all play the game, and when we dare,

| Dm7 | G7
To cheat ourselves at so - litaire

| Cm7 | Cm7
In - venting lovers on the phone,

| Cm7 Fm6 | Fm6 Fm7
Re - penting other lives un - known

| A♭ | G7
That call and say "Come dance with me"

| Cm7 | Fm6 Fm7 |
And murmur vague obscen - ities

| Dm7 | Dm7 | G7 | G7 ‖
At ugly girls like me, at seventeen.

Outro

| Cadd9 C Cmaj7 | C6 C | Cmaj9 ‖

rit.

BARBARA ALLEN

Traditional

Arranged by Peggy Seeger

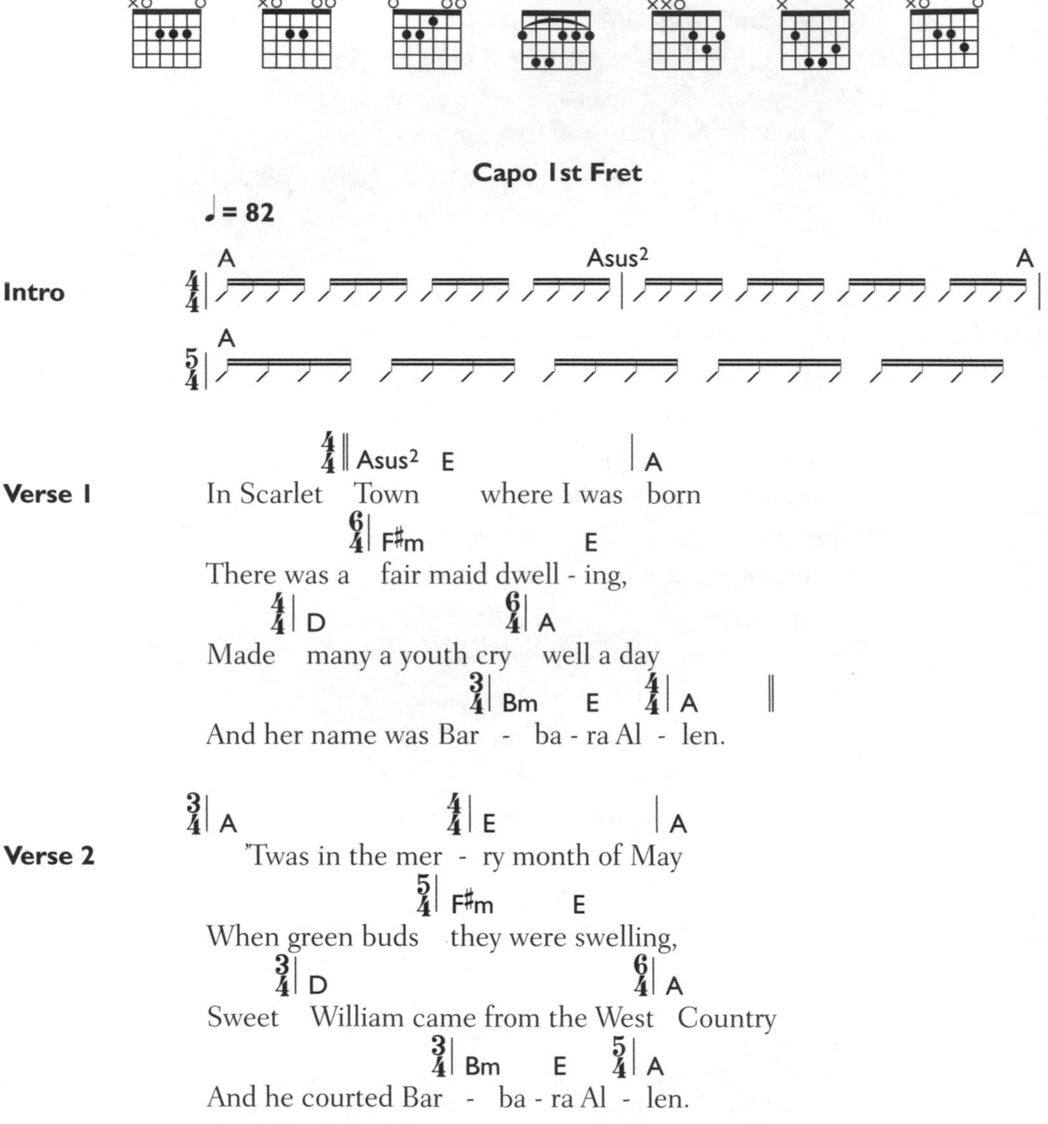

```
                    3|E         4|A
Verse 3   He sent his  servant unto  her,____
                          6|F#m          E
          To the place where  she was dwell - ing,
            4|D                 |A            |
          "My  master's sick, bids me  call for you
          3|A               |Bm E    4|A       ||
            If your name be Bar - bara Al - len."

          3|A        4|E           |A
Verse 4     Well slowly,  slowly got she  up
                    6|F#m      E
          And slowly  went she nigh him
            4|D              |A            |
          But  all she said as she  passed his bed
          |A             Bm  E     5|A
            "Young man I think you're dy - ing."

                    3|E           4|A
Verse 5   He turned his  pale face to the  wall,____
                    5|F#m     E
          And busted  out a cry - ing,
           4|D             |A          |
          "A - dieu, adieu my  dear friends all,
          |A           3|Bm E     4|A      ||
            Be kind to  Bar - bara Al - len."

          |A         E                 |A
Verse 6     Well lightly tripped she down the  stairs,
                        6|F#m        E
          She heard those  church bells tolling,
            4|D              6|A
          And  each bell seemed to  say as it tolled
                          3|Bm E     4|A     |
          "Hard hearted  Bar - bara All - en."
```

Verse 7

```
3/4| A        ‖ E                          4/4| A
   And she   looked East and she looked    West,
             5/4| F#m              E
She'd seen his   pale corpse a - coming,
  4/4| D                  6/4| A
"Lay   down, lay down that   corpse of clay
          4/4| Bm    E    | A          Asus4 | A  Asus2   | A  Asus2
That I may    look        u - pon him."
```

Verse 8

```
  6/4| A            E          4/4| A
Oh    mother, mo - ther go make my bed
       6/4| F#m            E
Go make it   long and nar - row,
   5/4| D              4/4| A         |
Sweet   William died for   me today
| A           | Bm  E       | A        ‖
   I'll die for  him      tomor - row.
```

Verse 9

```
‖ A               E             | E                        | A       |
   They buried    Sweet William   in the old church yard,
3/4| A                6/4| F#m      E
      They buried Bar - bara be - side him,
  4/4| D                    | A          |
Out   of his grave grew a    red, red rose
3/4| A            5/4| F#m  E   | A
      And out of     hers    a   briar.
```

Verse 10

```
                ‖ E                        | A
They grew and    grew up the old church   wall
              4/4| F#m     E    3/4| E
Till they could   grow no higher
  6/4| D                4/4| A         |
And   at the top twined in a  lovers knot
| A          6/4| Bm    E   4/4| A     | A        ‖
   The red rose   and     the   briar.
```

CLOSER TO FINE

Words and Music by Emily Saliers

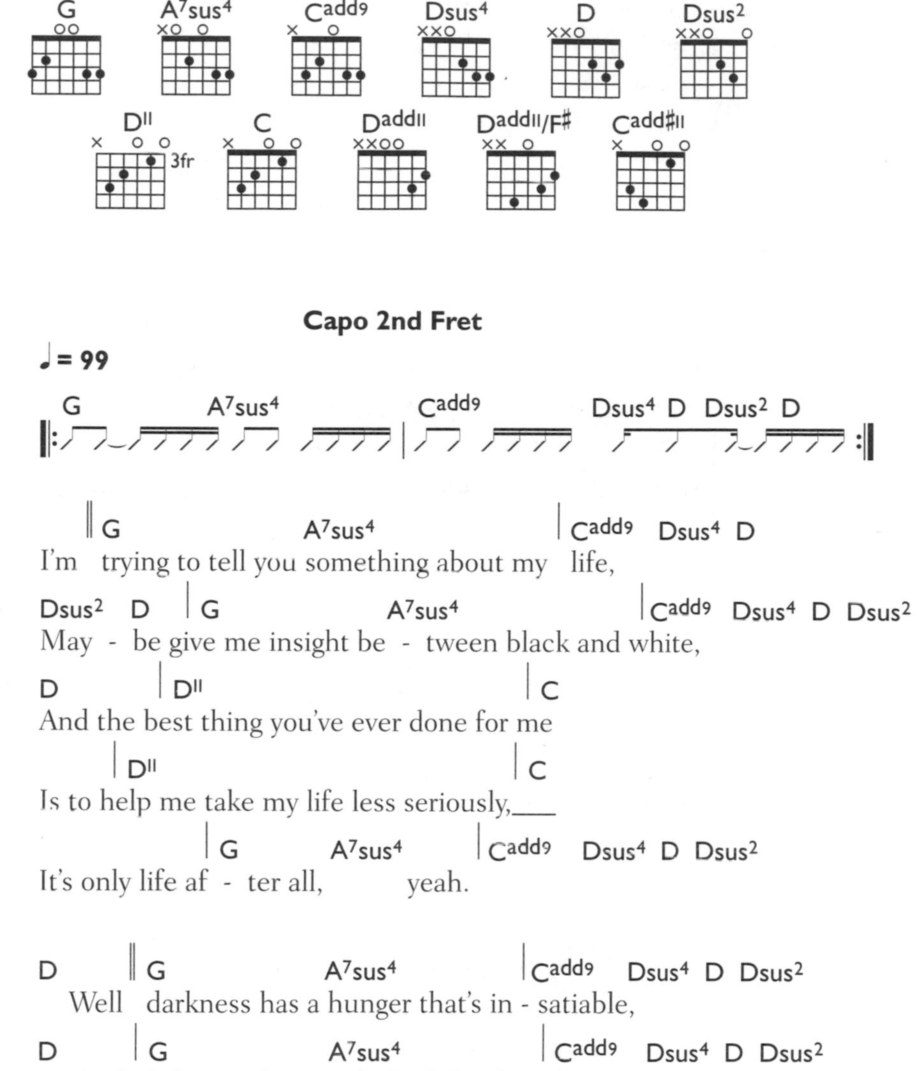

Capo 2nd Fret

♩ = 99

Intro

G A7sus4 | Cadd9 Dsus4 D Dsus2 D :||

Verse 1

|| G A7sus4 | Cadd9 Dsus4 D
I'm trying to tell you something about my life,

Dsus2 D | G A7sus4 | Cadd9 Dsus4 D Dsus2
May - be give me insight be - tween black and white,

D | D11 | C
And the best thing you've ever done for me

| D11 | C
Is to help me take my life less seriously,___

| G A7sus4 | Cadd9 Dsus4 D Dsus2
It's only life af - ter all, yeah.

Verse 2

D || G A7sus4 | Cadd9 Dsus4 D Dsus2
Well darkness has a hunger that's in - satiable,

D | G A7sus4 | Cadd9 Dsus4 D Dsus2
And lightness has a call that's hard to hear,

D | D11 | C
And I wrap my fear around me like a blanket,

| D11 | C
I sailed my ship of safety till I sank it,

| G
I'm crawling on your shores.

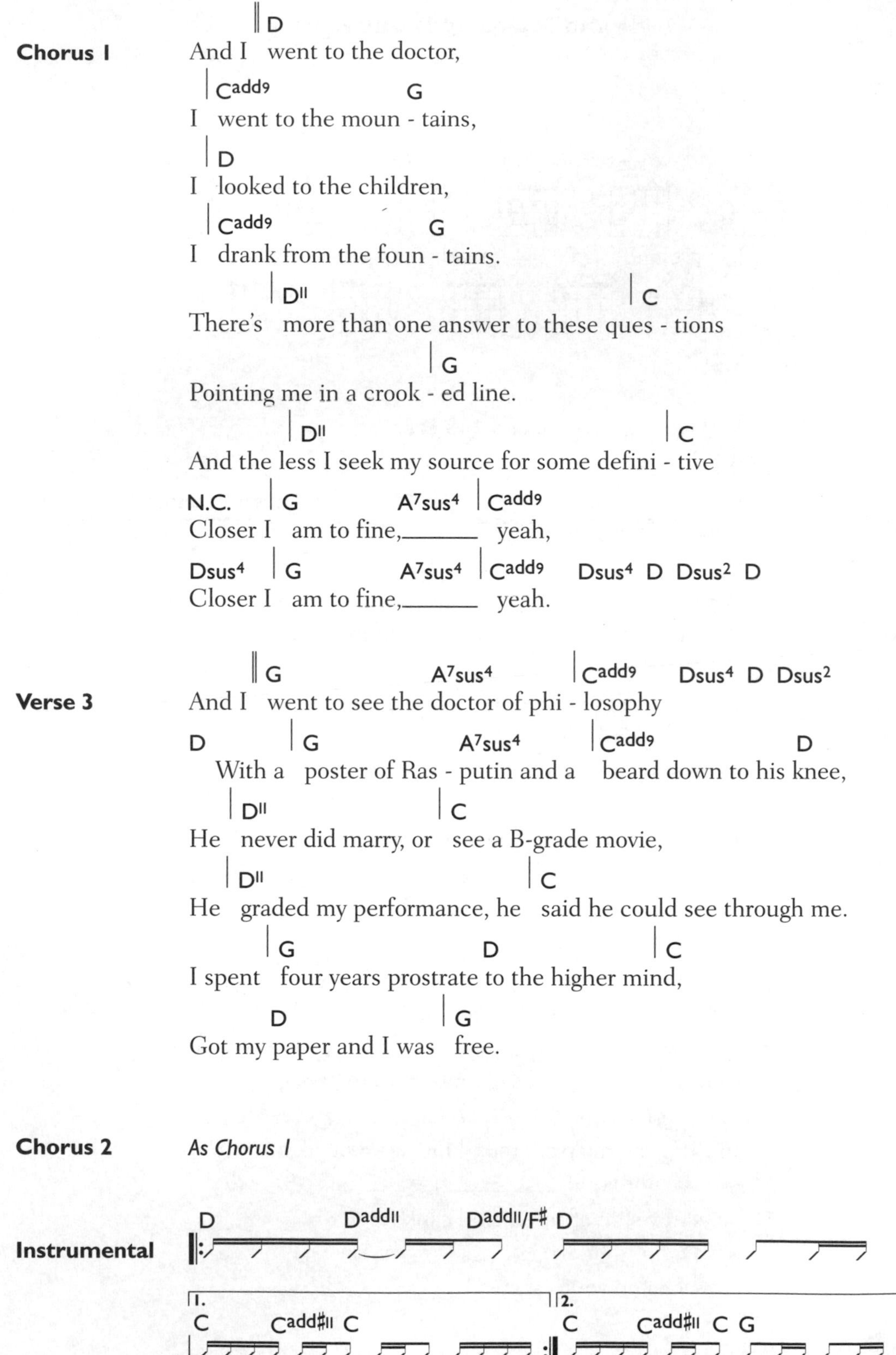
Chorus 1
D
And I went to the doctor,
Cadd9 G
I went to the moun - tains,
D
I looked to the children,
Cadd9 G
I drank from the foun - tains.
D11 C
There's more than one answer to these ques - tions
G
Pointing me in a crook - ed line.
D11 C
And the less I seek my source for some defini - tive
N.C. G A7sus4 Cadd9
Closer I am to fine, yeah,
Dsus4 G A7sus4 Cadd9 Dsus4 D Dsus2 D
Closer I am to fine, yeah.
Verse 3
G A7sus4 Cadd9 Dsus4 D Dsus2
And I went to see the doctor of phi - losophy
D G A7sus4 Cadd9 D
With a poster of Ras - putin and a beard down to his knee,
D11 C
He never did marry, or see a B-grade movie,
D11 C
He graded my performance, he said he could see through me.
G D C
I spent four years prostrate to the higher mind,
D G
Got my paper and I was free.
Chorus 2
As Chorus 1
Instrumental
D Dadd11 Dadd11/F# D
1.
C Cadd#11 C
2.
C Cadd#11 C G

Verse 4

‖ G A7sus4 | Cadd9 Dsus4 D
I stopped by the bar at three a. m.,

Dsus2 D | G A7sus4 | Cadd9 D
To seek solace in a bottle, or possibly a friend.

| D11 | C
And I woke up with a headache like my head against a board,

| D11 | C
Twice as cloudy as I'd been the night before,

| G
And I went in seeking cla - rity.

Chorus 3

‖ D | Cadd9 G
And I went to the doctor, I went to the mountains,

| D | Cadd9 G
I looked to the children, I drank from the fountain.

| D | Cadd9 G
We go to the doctor, we go to the mountains,

| D | Cadd9 G
We look to the children, we drink from the fountain.

| D | Cadd9 G
Yeah we go to the Bible, we go through the workout,

| D
We read up on revival,

| Cadd9 G
And we stand up for the look - out.

| D11 | C
There's more than one answer to these questions

| G
Pointing me in a crooked line,

| D11 | C
And the less I seek my source for some defini - tive,

N.C. | G A7sus4 | Cadd9
Closer I am to fine,__________

Dsus4 | G A7sus4 | Cadd9
Closer I am to fine,__________

Dsus4 | G A7sus4 | Cadd9 Dsus4 D Dsus2 D | G ‖
Closer I am to fine._______ yeah.

DANNY BOY

Traditional
Arranged by Eva Cassidy

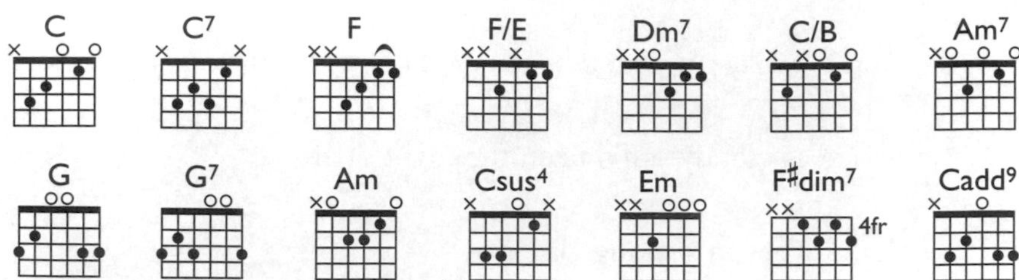

♩ = 76

Verse 1

‖ C | C | C7 | F F/E |
Oh Danny boy, the pipes, the pipes are calling

| Dm7 | C C/B | Am7 G | Dm7 |
From glen to glen, and down the mountain - side.

| G7 | C | C7 | F F/E |
The summer's gone and all the flowers dying

| Dm7 | C Am7 | Dm7 G | C Csus4 ‖
'Tis you, 'tis you must go and I must bide.

Chorus 1

| C G | C | F | C |
But come ye back when summer's in the meadow

| G | Am G | F Em | Dm7 |
Or when the val - ley's hushed and white with snow.

| G7 | C C/B | F F♯dim7 | C |
'Tis I'll be here in sunshine or in shadow

| F | C Am7 | Dm7 G | C Csus4 |
Oh Danny boy, oh Danny boy I love you so.

Verse 2

‖ G | Cadd9 | C7 | F F/E |
But when ye come and all the roses falling
| Dm7 | C C/B | Am7 G | Dm7 |
And I am dead, as dead I well may be
| G7 | C | C7 | F F/E |
Go out and find the place where I am lying
| Dm7 | C Am7 | Dm7 G | C Csus4 ‖
And kneel and say a 'Ave' there for me.

Chorus 2

| C G | C | F | C |
And I will hear 'tho soft your tread a - bove me
| G | Am G | F Em | Dm7 |
And then my grave will warm and sweeter be
| G7 | C F | F♯dim7 N.C. (fermata) | C *(freely)* C/B |
For you shall bend and tell me, that you love me
| F | C Am7 | Dm7 G7 | C Csus4 | C ‖
And I will sleep in peace until you come to me.

DAYS

Words and Music by Ray Davies

A E D F C G Am A7

♩ = 99

```
        A              A
Intro   4/4 | /          | /         ||

        | A                  | A     | E
Verse 1     Thank you for the days,___
              D    | A           D         A          E     |
        Those endless  days, those sacred days  you gave  me.
        | A                  | A     | E
            I'm thinking of the days,___
          D       | A   D    A       E     | A
        I won't for - get a single day be - lieve me.___
          D       | A
        I bless the light,
          D           | A       D       A      E     | A
        I bless the light  that lights on you be - lieve me.___
            D       | A
        And though you're  gone,
               D     | A    D      A      E    | A   ||
        You're with me every single day be - lieve me.___

        | F          C         | G      |
Chorus 1  Days I'll re - member all my  life,
        | F            C               | G
          Days, when you can't see wrong from   right,
             F   | C
        You took my__ life,
             F    | C        F  C        G    | C
        But then I  knew that very soon you'd leave me.__
             F  | C
        But it's al - right,
              F    | C          F      C      G    | C
        Now I'm not  frightened of this world be - lieve me.__
```

Bridge

‖E | Am
I wish today__ could be to - morrow,
| E
The night is long,
2/4 | Am G 4/4 | F
It just brings sorrow, let it wait.
| E
Ah.____

Verse 2

‖A | E
Thank you for the days,________
D | A D A E |
Those endless days, those sacred days you gave me.__
| A | A | E
I'm thinking of the days,________
D | A D A E | A ‖
I won't for - get a single day be - lieve me._____

Chorus 2

As Chorus 1

Link

‖ E | E
Days.____________________

Verse 3

As Verse 2

Outro

D ‖A
I bless the light
D | A D A E | A
I bless the light that lights on you, be - lieve me.
D | A
And though you're gone
D A D A E | A |
You're with me every single day be - lieve me.____
| A^7 | A^7 | A^7 | A^7 | $\overset{\frown}{A^7}$ ‖
Days.____________________

DIRTY OLD TOWN

Words and Music by Ewan MacColl

G/D G C D Em

♩ = 150 (swung quavers)

Intro

| G/D | G/D | G/D |
(banjo picking)

Verse 1

G/D I met my	G love	G by the gas works	G wall
G Dreamed a	C dream	C by the old ca -	G nal,
G Kissed my	G girl	G by the factory	G wall
G Dirty old	D town,
D C Dirty old	Em town.	Em	

Verse 2

G/D Clouds a -	G drift -	G ing across the	G moon,
G Cats are	C prowl -	C ing on their	G beat,
G Spring's a	G girl	G from the streets at	G night,
G Dirty old	D town,
D C Dirty old	Em town.	Em	

Verse 3

| G/D | G | G | G |
I heard a sir - en from the docks,
| G | C | C | G |
Saw a train set the night on fire,
| G | G | G | G |
Smelled the spring on the smoky wind,
| G | D |
Dirty old town,
| D C | Em | Em ||
Dirty old town.

Verse 4

| G/D | G | G | G |
I'm going to make a good sharp axe,
| G | C | C | G |
Shining steel tempered in the fire,
| G | G | G | G |
I'll chop you down like an old dead tree,
| G | D |
Dirty old town,
| D C | Em | Em ||
Dirty old town.

Verse 5

| G/D | G | G | G |
I met my love by the factory wall,
| G | C | C | G |
Dreamed a dream by the old ca - nal,
| G | G | G | G |
Kissed my girl by the factory wall,
| G | D |
Dirty old town,
| D C | Em |
Dirty old town,
| Em | D |
Dirty old town,
| D | G |
Dirty old town.

G
| 𝅗𝅥 𝅗𝅥 ||

DIAMONDS AND RUST

Words and Music by Joan Baez

Em Em/F♯ (4fr) Em/G (5fr) Em/A (7fr) Em/B Am⁹/B (5fr) B⁷/A B⁷/D♯

B⁷ Em⁹ C G D Bm⁷ Am⁷ Fmaj⁷

Capo 1st Fret

♩ = 130

Intro

4/4 | Em Em/F♯ Em | Em Em/F♯ Em Em/F♯ |
Em/G Em/F♯ Em/G	Em/A Em/G Em/A	Em/B
Am⁹/B	Em/B	B⁷/A B⁷/D♯	B⁷
Em Em/F♯ Em	Em Em/F♯ Em

Verse 1

‖ Em | Em⁹ | C | C
Well I'll be damn - ed here comes your ghost again___
| G | G
But that's not un - usual,
| D |
It's just that the moon is full
| D | Em | Em⁹
And you happened to call.
| Em | Em⁹ | C | C
And here I sit hand on the telephone,___
| G | G
Hearing a voice I'd known___
| D |
A couple of light years ago___
| D | Em | Em⁹ | Em | Em⁹
Heading straight for a fall.

Verse 2

```
   ‖ Em                         | Em9                  | C             | C
As   I remember your eyes     were bluer than   Robins' eggs,___
                    | G                  | G
My poetry was   lousy you said,___
                      | D               |
Where are you call - ing from?
| D                    | Em          | Em9        |
    A booth in the   Midwest.
| Em                 | Em9                        | C                   |
    Ten years ago     I bought you some     cufflinks,___
| C                      | G            | G
    You brought me   something___
                        | D                        |
We both know what   memories can bring,
| D                                      | Em         | Em/F#    ‖
    They bring diamonds and   rust.
```

Instrumental I

```
Em/G      Em/F#      Em/G  Em/A      Em/G      Em/A  Em/B
|/ / /   / / /   / / | / / /   / / /   / / | / / /   / / /   / / |
Am9/B                Em/B                 B7/A               B7/D#  B7
|/ / /   / / /   / / | / / /   / / /   / / | / / /   / / /   / / | / / / /   / / / / |
Em                   Em/F#  Em            Em                  Em/F#  Em
|/ / /   / / /   / / | / / /   / / /   / / | / / /   / / /   / / | / / /   / / /   / /
```

Verse 3

```
     ‖ Em                              | Em9             | C          |
Well   you burst on the scene     already a   legend,
| C                    | G                 |
    The unwashed   phenomenon,
| G                | D              |
    The original   vagabond,
| D                             | Em          | Em9
    You strayed into my   arms.
    | Em                   | Em9                  | C                   |
And   there you stayed     temporarily   lost at sea,
| C                           | G                       |
    The Madonna was   yours for free,
| G                           | D                      |
    Yes, the girl on the   half shell
| D                           | Em          | Em9          | Em          | Em9
    could keep you un - harmed.
```

Bridge

| Bm^7
Now I see you standing

| Bm^7 | Am^7 | Am^7
With brown leaves falling around, and snow in your hair.____

| Bm^7
Now you're smil - ing out the window

| Bm^7 | Am^7 | Am^7
Of that crummy ho - tel over Washington Square.____

| C | C | G | G
Our breath comes out white clouds, mingles and hangs in the air.

| Fmaj^7 | Fmaj^7 | G | G
Speaking strictly for me, we both could have died then and there.

Instrumental 2

| B^7 | Em/B | Am^9/B |

| Em/B | B^7/A B^7/D$^\sharp$ | B^7 |

| Em | Em/F$^\sharp$ Em | Em | Em/F$^\sharp$ Em

Verse 4

|| Em | Em^9 | C |
Now you're telling me you're not nos - talgic,____

| C | G | G
Then give me another word for it,____

| D
You who are so good with words,____

| Em | Em^9
And at keeping things vague.

| Em | Em^9
'Cause I need some of that vagueness now,

| C |
It's all come back too clearly,

| C | G |
Yes I loved you dearly,

| G | D |
And if you're offering me diamonds and rust

| D | Em | Em^9 | Em | Em^9 |
I've already paid.

Outro

|: Em | Em^9 :| *Repeat to fade*

EVERYTHING YOU NEED

Words and Music by Adem Ilhan

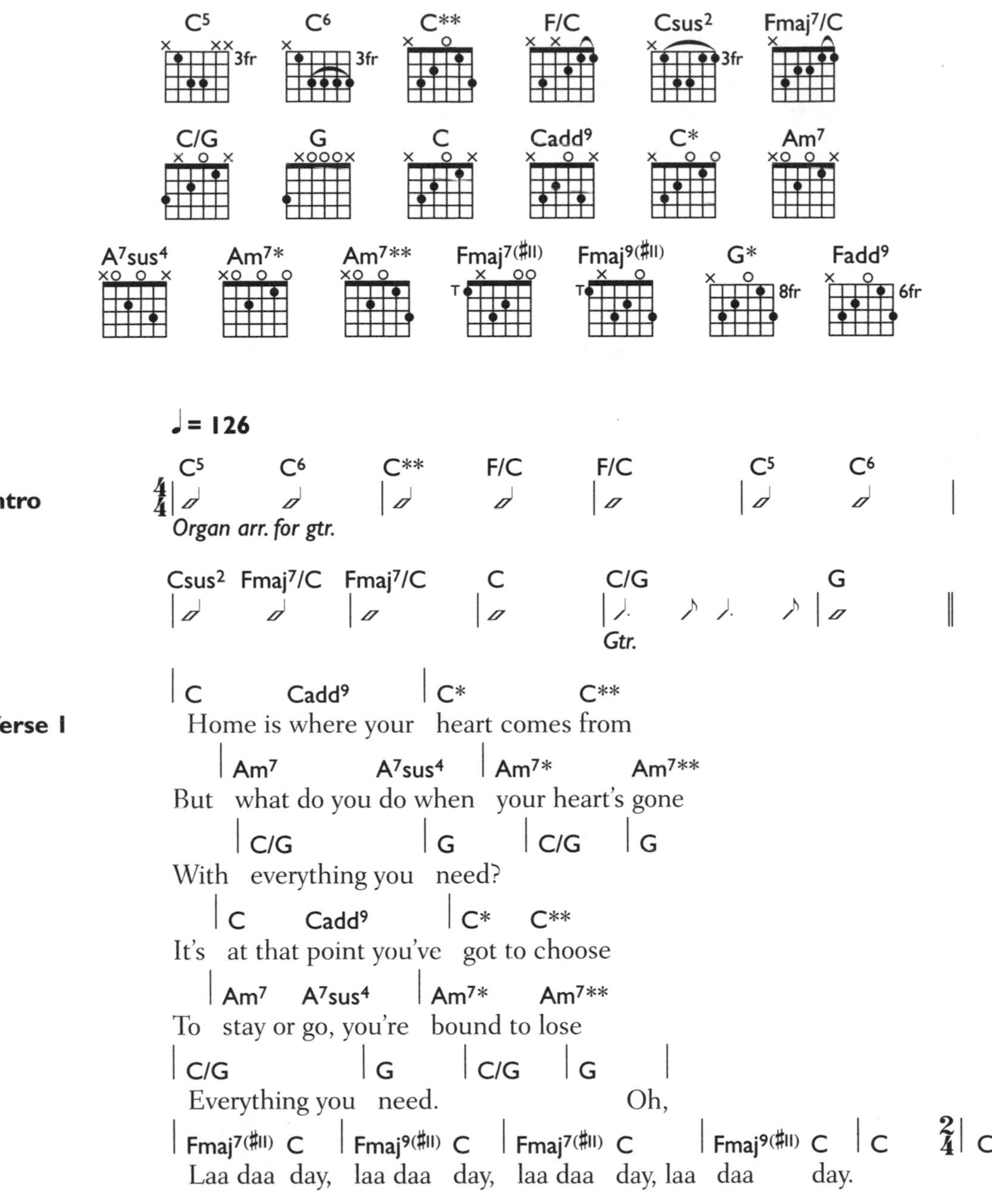
C5 C6 C** F/C Csus2 Fmaj7/C
3fr 3fr 3fr
C/G G C Cadd9 C* Am7
A7sus4 Am7* Am7** Fmaj7(♯11) Fmaj9(♯11) G* Fadd9
8fr 6fr
♩= 126
Intro
C5 C6 C** F/C F/C C5 C6
Organ arr. for gtr.
Csus2 Fmaj7/C Fmaj7/C C C/G G
Gtr.
Verse 1
C Cadd9 C* C**
Home is where your heart comes from
Am7 A7sus4 Am7* Am7**
But what do you do when your heart's gone
C/G G C/G G
With everything you need?
C Cadd9 C* C**
It's at that point you've got to choose
Am7 A7sus4 Am7* Am7**
To stay or go, you're bound to lose
C/G G C/G G
Everything you need. Oh,
Fmaj7(♯11) C Fmaj9(♯11) C Fmaj7(♯11) C Fmaj9(♯11) C C C
Laa daa day, laa daa day, laa daa day, laa daa day.

Verse 2

```
  4/4 | C        Cadd9   | C*        C**
You    got your stuff you  packed your bags
     | Am7          A7sus4     | Am7*    Am7** |
You    checked your things made  sure you had
| C/G            | G      | C/G     | G
  Everything you   need
     | C        Cadd9   | C*          C**
You    upped, you left, you  went away____
     | Am7    A7sus4 | Am7*    Am7**
To   love to fight an - other day____
        | C/G              | G      | C/G     | G        |
'Gainst      everything you   need.                Oh,
| Fmaj7(#11) C  | Fmaj9(#11) C | Fmaj7(#11) C  | Fmaj9(#11) C | C  | C
  Laa daa   day, laa   daa    day,  laa daa   day, laa  daa     day.______
```

Chorus 1

```
|| G*       | G*                 | Fadd9
  Ooh, you    severed your ties____
     | Fadd9        | Am7*
You    left us all be - hind
     | Am7*          | Fadd9
You    said all your good - byes
    | Fadd9          | G*
To    everything you   need
     | G*               | Fadd9
You    severed your ties____
    | Fadd9             | Am7*
Re - forge them make it   right
        | Am7*          | Fadd9
Come      back with open   eyes
    | Fadd9          | C**       | C**     ||
To    everything you   need.___________
```

Instrumental

Am7** //// //// //// ////	Am7** //// //// //// ////
C** //// //// //// ////	C** //// //// //// ////
Am7** //// //// //// ////	Am7** //// //// //// ////

Verse 3

```
        ‖ C          Cadd9    | C*     C**
'Cause    moments they can    turn to dreams
     | Am7        A7sus4      | Am7*        Am7**
And    hopes and wants can     sometimes seem
     | C/G             | G     | C/G   | G
Like   everything you   need.
    | C        Cadd9    | C*     C**
But   treated bad then    left a - lone
    | Am7       A7sus4  | Am7*       Am7**
You   cried, we said to   come back home
   | C/G            | G      | C/G    | G      |
To   everything you   need.                  Oh,
| Fmaj7(#11) C      | Fmaj9(#11) C    | Fmaj7(#11) C     | Fmaj9(#11) C  | C    2/4 | C
  Laa daa  day, laa   daa       day,    laa daa  day, laa   daa    day.________
```

Chorus 2

As Chorus 1

Outro

‖ Am7** //// //// //// //// | Am7** //// //// //// //// |
| C** //// //// //// //// | C** //// //// //// //// |
| Am7** //// //// //// //// | Am7** //// //// //// //// ‖

to fade

A FATHER AND A SON

Words and Music by Loudon Wainwright III

G D Em C Am Bm

Capo 7th Fret

♩= 163

Intro 4/4 | G | D Em | C G |
| G | G | G | G |

Verse 1

G D Em
When I was your age I was just like you,
C G
And just look at me now; I'm sure you do.
G D Em
But your grandfather was just as bad
C G
And you should have heard him trash his dad.
G D
Life's no picnic, that's a given:
C G
My mom's mom died when my mom was seven;
G D Em
My mom's father was a tragic guy,
C G G G
But he was so distant and no - body knows why.
G Am Bm Bm Bm Bm
Now, your mother's family, you know them:
C G
Each and every one a gem,
C G
Each and every one a gem.

Verse 2

‖ G | D Em
When I was your age I was a mess;
| C | G |
On a bad day I still am, I guess.
| G | D Em
I think I know what you're going through;
| C | G
Everything changes but nothing is new.
| G | D
And I know that I'm miserable; can't you see?
| C | G
I just want you to be just like me.
| G | D Em
Boys grow up to be grown men
| C | G | G | G | G
And then men change back into boys again.
| Am | Bm | Bm | Bm | Bm
You're starting up and I'm winding down;____
| C | G |
Ain't it big enough for us both in this town?
| C | G ‖
Say it's big enough for us both in this town.

Link

‖: G | D Em | C |
| G :‖ G | G ‖

Verse 3

‖ G | G | D Em
When I was your age I thought I hated my dad
| C | G |
And that the feeling was a mutual one that we had;
| G | D Em
We fought each other day and night:
| C | G
I was always wrong; and he was always right.
| G | D
But he had the power, he needed to win;
| C | G |
His life half over, mine a - bout to begin.

cont.

```
| G                          | D       Em
  I'm not sure about that   Oedipal stuff,
           | C                          | G         | G   | G   | G   |
But when   we were together it was al - ways rough.
| Am                      | Bm            | Bm    | Bm    | Bm
  Hate is a strong word;    I wanna back - track;
     | C                     | G
The  bigger the front, the   bigger the back;
     | C                     | G
The  bigger the front, the   bigger the back.
```

Verse 4

```
     || G                | D          Em
Now     you and me are     me and you,
            | C                            | G                |
And it's a    different ballgame though     not brand-new.
| G                              | D        Em
  I don't know what all of this    fighting is for;
        | C                         | G              |
We're     having us a teenage/mid - dle-age war.
| G                         | D
  I don't wanna die and       you want to live;
            | C                         | G
It takes a    little bit of take and a    whole lot of give.
   | G                            | D             Em
It    never really ends though      each race is run,
     | C                    | G                  | G     | G     | G     |
This      thing between a     father and a son.
| Am                | Bm         | Bm      | Bm      | Bm      |
  Maybe it's power     push and    shove,
| C                  | G                |
  Maybe it's hate but  probably it's love,
| C                  | G                ||
  Maybe it's hate but  probably it's love.
```

Outro

```
                                                                         rit.
  G                    D     Em             C                      G
| / / / / _ / / / /  | / / / / _ / / / /  | / / / / _ / / / /  | / / /  𝅗𝅥  ||
```

FISHERMAN'S BLUES

Words and Music by Stephen Wickham and Michael Scott

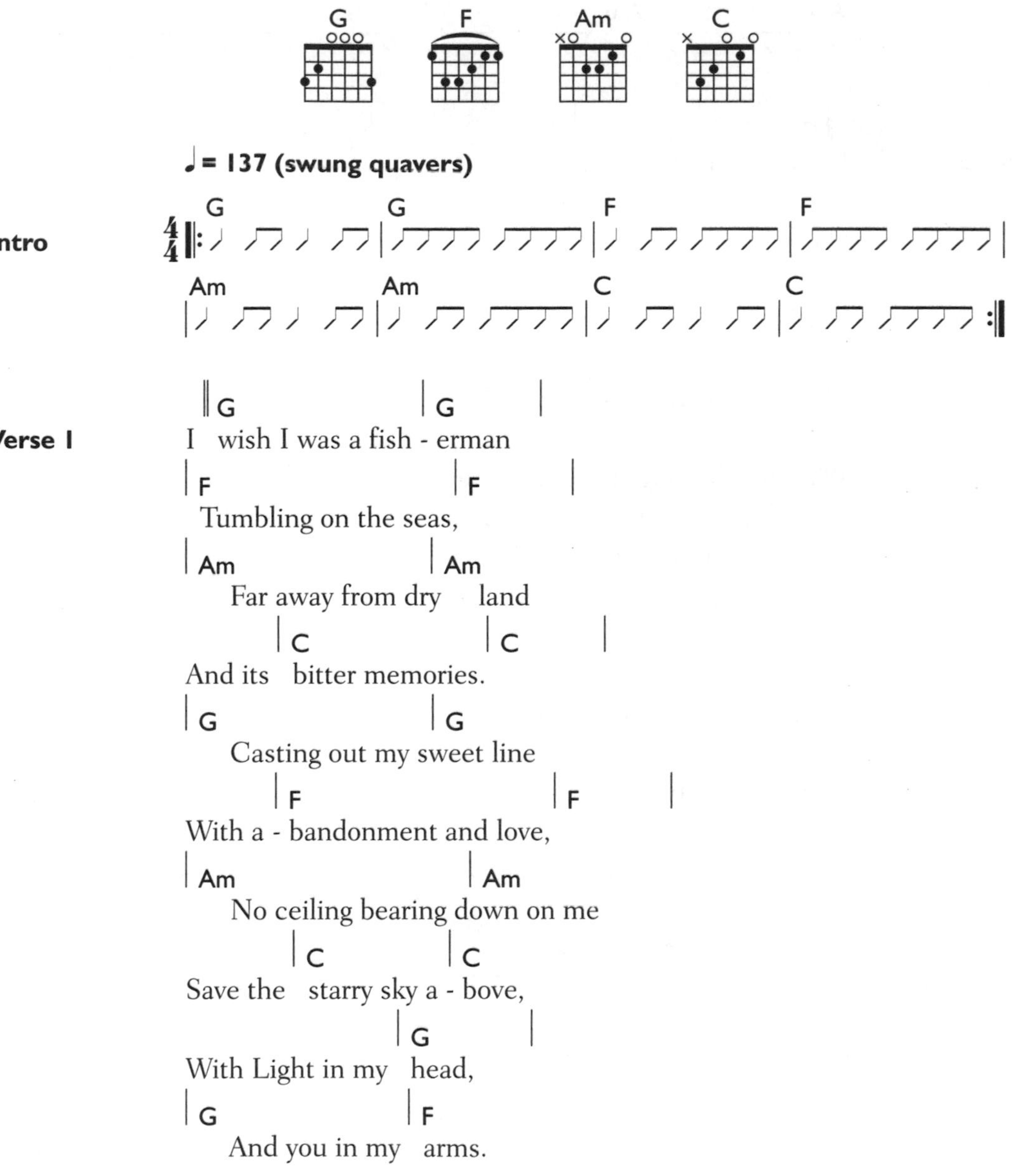
G F Am C
♩ = 137 (swung quavers)
Intro
G G F F
Am Am C C
Verse 1
G G
I wish I was a fish - erman
F F
Tumbling on the seas,
Am Am
Far away from dry land
C C
And its bitter memories.
G G
Casting out my sweet line
F F
With a - bandonment and love,
Am Am
No ceiling bearing down on me
C C
Save the starry sky a - bove,
G
With Light in my head,
G F
And you in my arms.

Instrumental 1

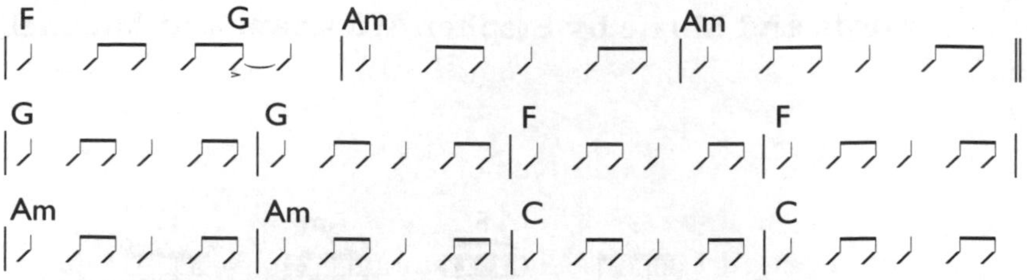

| F G | Am | Am ||
| G | G | F | F |
| Am | Am | C | C

Verse 2

|| G | G
I wish I was the brake - man
| F | F
On a hurtling, fevered train,
| Am | Am
Crashing headlong into the heart - land
| C | C
Like a cannon in the rain.
| G | G
With the beating of the sleep - ers
| F | F
And the burning of the coal,
| Am | Am
Count - ing the towns flashing by
| C | C
In a night that's full of soul,
| G
With Light in my head
| G | F |
And you in my arms.

Instrumental 2

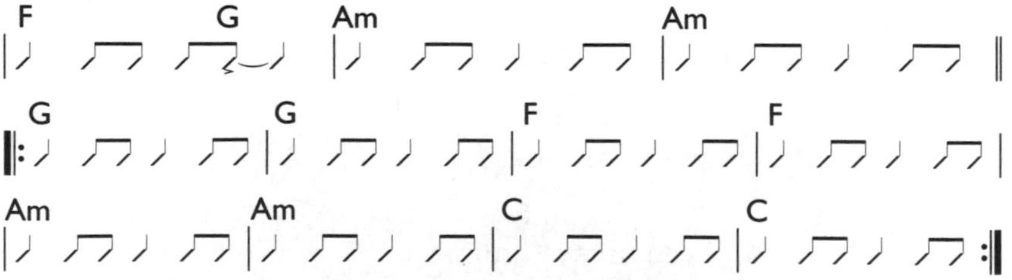

F G	Am	Am	
: G	G	F	F
Am	Am	C	C :

Verse 3
G G
I know I will be loos - ened
F F
From the bonds that hold me fast,
Am Am
That the chains all hung around me
C C
Will fall away at last.
G G
And on that fine and fateful day
F F
I will take me in my hands,
Am Am
I will ride on the train
C C
I will be the fisher - man
G
With Light in my head
G F
And you in my arms.
Instrumental 3
F G Am Am C C
Outro
G G F F
Am Am C C
Repeat ad lib. to fade

FINNEGAN'S WAKE

Traditional

Arranged by Christy Moore

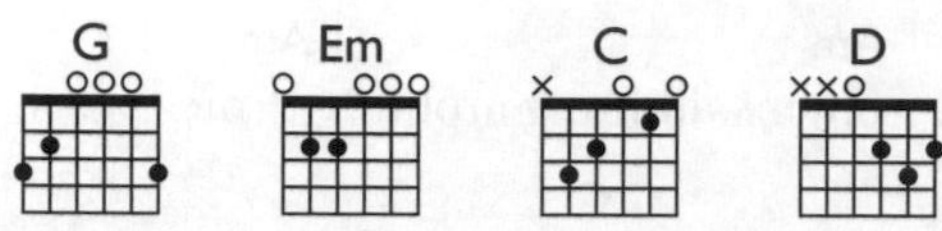

Capo 1st Fret

♩ = 96

free time *a tempo*

Verse 1

| G 4/4 | G Em
Oh Tim Finnegan lived in Walkin Street,
| C D
A gentleman Irish mighty odd,
| G Em
He'd a beautiful brogue so rich and sweet,
3/4 | C D 4/4 | G
An' to rise in the world he carried a hod.
| G Em
But you see he'd a kind of a tippling way,
| C D
With a love for the liquor Tim was born,
| G Em
To help him at his work each day,
| C D G ||
He'd a drop of the craythur every morn.

Chorus 1

| G Em |
Whack fol the dah now swing to yer partners,
| C D |
Well to the floor yer trotters shake,
| G Em |
Wasn't it the truth I told you?
3/4 | C D 4/4 | G
Lots of fun at Finnegan's Wake.

Verse 2

```
    ‖G                Em
One   morning Tim was rather full,
    |C                  D
His   head felt heavy and it made him shake,
   |G                         Em
He   fell from the ladder and he broke his skull,
        |C                  D        G
So they   took him home his corpse to wake.
     |G                     Em
They   wrapped him up in a nice clean sheet,
         |C               D
And they   laid him out upon    the bed,
        |G            Em
With a   bottle of porter at his feet
       |C                 D        G   ‖
And a   gallon of whiskey at his head.
```

Chorus 2 *As Chorus 1*

Verse 3

```
     ‖G                 Em
With   all his friends there at the wake,
    |C                    D          |
Mrs   Finnegan called out for the lunch
|G                 Em
  First they laid on tea and cake,
      |C                           D       G   |
Then   pipes and tobacco and whiskey punch
|G                  Em
  Biddy O'Brien be - gan to cry,
         |C                      D       |
"Such a   pretty corpse, did you ever see,
|G                 Em
  Tim me love, why did you die?"
          |C                       D        G  ‖
"Will ye   shut your mouth?" says Judy Mc - Gee.
```

Chorus 3 *As Chorus 1*

Verse 4

‖ G Em
Then Peggy Jordon took up the job,
| C D
"You're a Biddy" says she "you're wrong, I'm sure."
| G Em
But Biddy gave her a belt in the gob
| C D G
That left her sprawling on the floor
| G Em
Each side in war did then engage,
| C D |
'Twas woman for woman and man for man,
| G Em
Shill - elagh law was all the rage
| C D G ‖
And a row and a ruction soon began.

Chorus 4

As Chorus 1

Verse 5

‖ G Em
Well Mickey Mulvaney ducked his head
| C D
When a bottle of whiskey flew at him
| G Em
It missed him and scattered and on the bed,
$\frac{3}{4}$ | C D $\frac{4}{4}$ | G
The whiskey split all over Tim
| G Em |
By God he revives, see how he rises,
| G D
Timothy leaping up out from the bed
| G Em |
Cried while he lathered 'round like blazes,
| C D G ‖
"T'underin' Jaysus, do ye think I'm dead?"

Chorus 4

```
  | G                    Em              |
    Whack fol the dah now swing to yer partners
  | C                D          |
    Well to the floor yer trotters shake
  | G          Em          |
    Wasn't it the truth I told you?
3/4| C          D     2/4| G          |
    Lots of fun at Finnegan's  Wake.
4/4| G                    Em              |
    Whack fol the dah now swing to yer partners
  | C                D          |
    Well to the floor yer trotters shake,
  | G          Em          |
    Wasn't it the truth I told you?
3/4| C          D     4/4| G(fermata)  ||
    Lots of fun at Finnegan's  Wake.
```

FLAME TURNS BLUE

Words and Music by David Gray

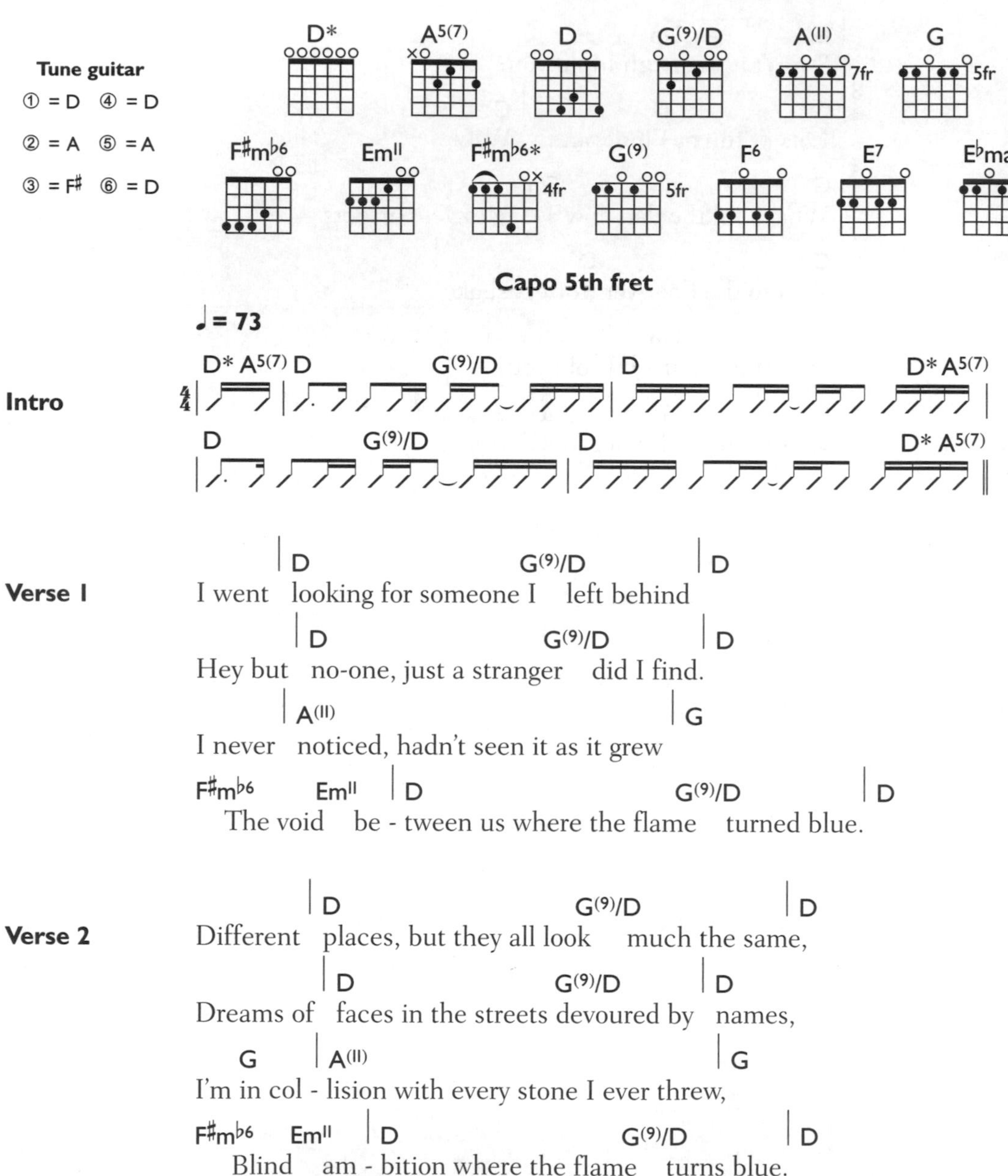
Tune guitar
① = D ④ = D
② = A ⑤ = A
③ = F♯ ⑥ = D
D* A5(7) D G(9)/D A(II) G
F♯m♭6 EmII F♯m♭6* G(9) F6 E7 E♭maj7
7fr 5fr 4fr 5fr
Capo 5th fret
♩ = 73
Intro
D* A5(7) D G(9)/D D D* A5(7)
D G(9)/D D D* A5(7)
Verse 1
D G(9)/D D
I went looking for someone I left behind
D G(9)/D D
Hey but no-one, just a stranger did I find.
A(II) G
I never noticed, hadn't seen it as it grew
F♯m♭6 EmII D G(9)/D D
The void be - tween us where the flame turned blue.
Verse 2
D G(9)/D D
Different places, but they all look much the same,
D G(9)/D D
Dreams of faces in the streets devoured by names,
G A(II) G
I'm in col - lision with every stone I ever threw,
F♯m♭6 EmII D G(9)/D D
Blind am - bition where the flame turns blue.

Verse 3

```
         | D              G(9)/D           | D
Words dis - mantled and all   the books unbound,
           | D                   G(9)/D      | D
Conver - sation, though we utter    not a sound.
  G        | A(11)                         | G   F#m♭6
I heard a   rumour, I don't know if it's true
Em11     | D                    G(9)/D      | D          ||
That you'd  meet me when the flame   turns blue,    alright now...
```

Instrumental

```
| D              G(9)/D          | D                       D* A5(7) |
| D              G(9)/D          | D                       G        |
| A(11)                          | G              F#m♭6    Em11     |
| D              G(9)/D          | D                                ||
```

Verse 4

```
      | D                       G(9)/D      | D
So I   venture underneath the leaden sky,
          | D                    G(9)/D      | D
See the   freight train with it's one   fierce eye.
    G       | A(11)                         | G    F#m♭6
And then I   listen as it tears the night in   two
Em11          | D               G(9)/D      | D
With a whis - tle and the flame   turns bluc.
```

Chorus 1

```
                                   || F#m♭6*  | G(9)     | A(11)   G(9) |
In the morning I will sing,
| D                                 | F#m♭6*  | G(9)     | A(11)   G(9) ||
   In the morning I will sing.
```

Verse 5

| D | D G(9)/D | D
Through the lemon trees, the dia - monds of light

| D G(9)/D | D
Break in splinters on the pages where I write,

G | A(11) | G
That if I lost you, I don't know what I'd do,

F#mb6 Em11 | D G(9)/D | D
Burn for - ever where the flame turns blue.

| A(11) | G
Yeah, if I lost you, I don't know what I'd do,

F#mb6 Em11 | D G(9)/D | D
Burn for - ever where the flame turns blue.

Chorus 2

|| F#mb6* | G(9) | A(11) G(9) |
In the morning I will sing,_________

| D | F#mb6* | G(9) | A(11) G(9) |
In the morning I will sing,

| D | F#mb6* | G(9) | A(11) G(9) |
In the morning I will sing,____ woah.

| D | F#mb6* | G(9) | A(11) G(9) | D ||
Sing.______

Outro

rit.

G(9) F6 | E7 Ebmaj7 | D A5(7) G(9)/D | D* ||

FROM BOTH SIDES NOW

Words and Music by Joni Mitchell

Tune guitar

① = D ④ = D

② = A ⑤ = A

③ = F# ⑥ = D

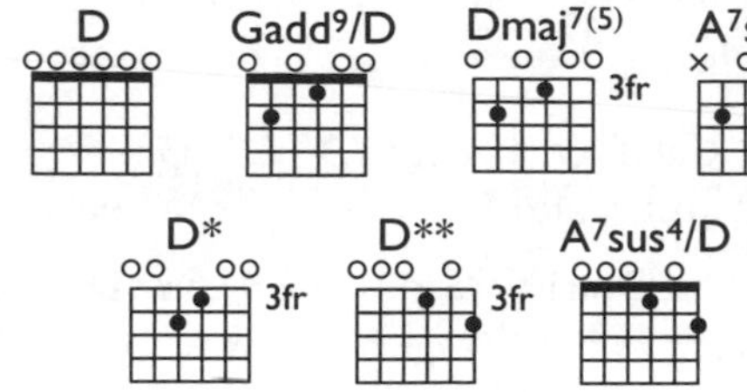

D Gadd9/D Dmaj7(5) 3fr A7sus4 3fr

D* 3fr D** 3fr A7sus4/D

Capo 4th Fret

♩= c. 94

Intro 4/4 D Gadd9/D D (D) Gadd9/D D

Verse I

Dmaj7(5) Gadd9/D | A7sus4/D D* D
Rows and flows of an - gel hair

Gadd9/D | D Dmaj7(5) Gadd9/D | A7sus4/D D** A7sus4/D D
And ice cream castles in the air

| Dmaj7(5) Gadd9/D | A7sus4/D |
And feather canyons everywhere

| Dmaj7(5) Gadd9/D | A7sus4/D
I've looked at clouds that way.

| Dmaj7(5) Gadd9/D | A7sus4/D D* D
But now they only block the sun

Gadd9/D | D Dmaj7(5) Gadd9/D | A7sus4/D D* A7sus4/D D
They rain and snow on every - one

| Dmaj7(5) Gadd9/D | A7sus4/D
So many things I would have done

| Dmaj7(5) Gadd9/D | A7sus4/D
But clouds got in my way.

Chorus I

|| D** A7sus4/D | A7sus4/D D
I've looked at clouds from both sides now,

| D** A7sus4/D D | A7sus4/D
From up and down, and still somehow

D | Dmaj7(5) Gadd9/D | D Gadd9/D D
It's cloud ill - usions I re - call

| Dmaj7(5) Gadd9/D D | A7sus4/D | A7sus4/D ||
I really don't know clouds at

Link 1

| D . . Gadd⁹/D . . D | (D) Dmaj⁷⁽⁵⁾ D Gadd⁹/D D |
all.

| D . . Gadd⁹/D . D | (D) . . Gadd⁹/D D ||

Verse 2

| Dmaj⁷⁽⁵⁾ Gadd⁹/D | A⁷sus⁴/D D* D
Moons and Junes and Fer - ris wheels
Gadd⁹/D | D Dmaj⁷⁽⁵⁾ Gadd⁹/D | A⁷sus⁴/D D*
The dizzy danc - ing way you feel
| Dmaj⁷⁽⁵⁾ Gadd⁹/D | A⁷sus⁴/D |
As ev'ry fairy - tale comes real
| Dmaj⁷⁽⁵⁾ Gadd⁹/D | A⁷sus⁴/D |
I've looked at love that way.____
| Dmaj⁷⁽⁵⁾ Gadd⁹/D | A⁷sus⁴/D D* D
But now it's just a - no - ther show
| Dmaj⁷⁽⁵⁾ Gadd⁹/D | A⁷sus⁴/D D*
You leave 'em laughing when you go
| Dmaj⁷⁽⁵⁾ Gadd⁹/D | A⁷sus⁴/D |
And if you care, don't let them know
Dmaj⁷⁽⁵⁾ | Gadd⁹/D | A⁷sus⁴/D
Don't give yourself away.

Chorus 2

|| D** A⁷sus⁴/D | Gadd⁹/D D
I've looked at love from both sides now,
| Gadd⁹/D D | Gadd⁹/D D
From give and take, and still some - how
| Dmaj⁷⁽⁵⁾ Gadd⁹/D | A⁷sus⁴/D
It's love's ill - usions I recall
| Dmaj⁷⁽⁵⁾ Gadd⁹/D D | A⁷sus⁴/D | A⁷sus⁴/D ||
I really don't know love____ at (all).

Link 2

As link 1

Verse 3

|| Dmaj⁷⁽⁵⁾ Gadd⁹/D | A⁷sus⁴/D D
Tears and fears and feeling proud
Gadd⁹/D | D Dmaj⁷⁽⁵⁾ Gadd⁹/D | A⁷sus⁴/D D* |
To say "I love you" right out loud.
| Dmaj⁷⁽⁵⁾ Gadd⁹/D | A⁷sus⁴/D |
Dreams and schemes and circus crowds
| Dmaj⁷⁽⁵⁾ Gadd⁹/D | A⁷sus⁴/D
I've looked at life that way.

cont.

| Dmaj$^{7(5)}$ Gadd^9/D | A^{7}sus^4/D D
But now old friends are acting strange
| Dmaj$^{7(5)}$ Gadd^9/D | A^{7}sus^4/D D*
They shake their heads, they say I've changed,
| Dmaj$^{7(5)}$ Gadd^9/D | A^{7}sus^4/D
Well something's lost but something's gained
| Dmaj$^{7(5)}$ Gadd^9/D | A^{7}sus^4
In living every - day.

Chorus 3

‖ D** A^{7}sus^4/D | Gadd^9/D D
I've looked at life from both sides now,
| Gadd^9/D D | Gadd^9/D D
From win and lose, and still some - how
| Dmaj$^{7(5)}$ Gadd^9/D | A^{7}sus^4/D
It's life's ill - usions I recall
| Dmaj$^{7(5)}$ Gadd^9/D D | A^{7}sus^4/D | A^{7}sus^4/D ‖
I really don't know life_____ at (all).

Link 3

As link 1

Chorus 4

‖ D** A^{7}sus^4/D | Gadd^9/D D
I've looked at life from both sides now,
| Gadd^9/D D | Gadd^9/D D
From up and down, and still some - how
| Dmaj$^{7(5)}$ Gadd^9/D | A^{7}sus^4/D
It's life's ill - usions I recall
| Dmaj$^{7(5)}$ Gadd^9/D D | A^{7}sus^4/D | A^{7}sus^4/D ‖
I really don't know life_______ at

Outro

| D Gadd^9/D D | (D) Dmaj$^{7(5)}$ D Gadd^9/D D | D Gadd^9/D D |
all.
| D Gadd^9/D D | D Gadd^9/D D | D Gadd^9/D D |
| D Gadd^9/D D | (D) Dmaj$^{7(5)}$ D Gadd^9/D D |
| D Gadd^9/D D | (D) ‖

THE GALWAY FARMER

Words and Music by Steve Knightley and Philip Beer

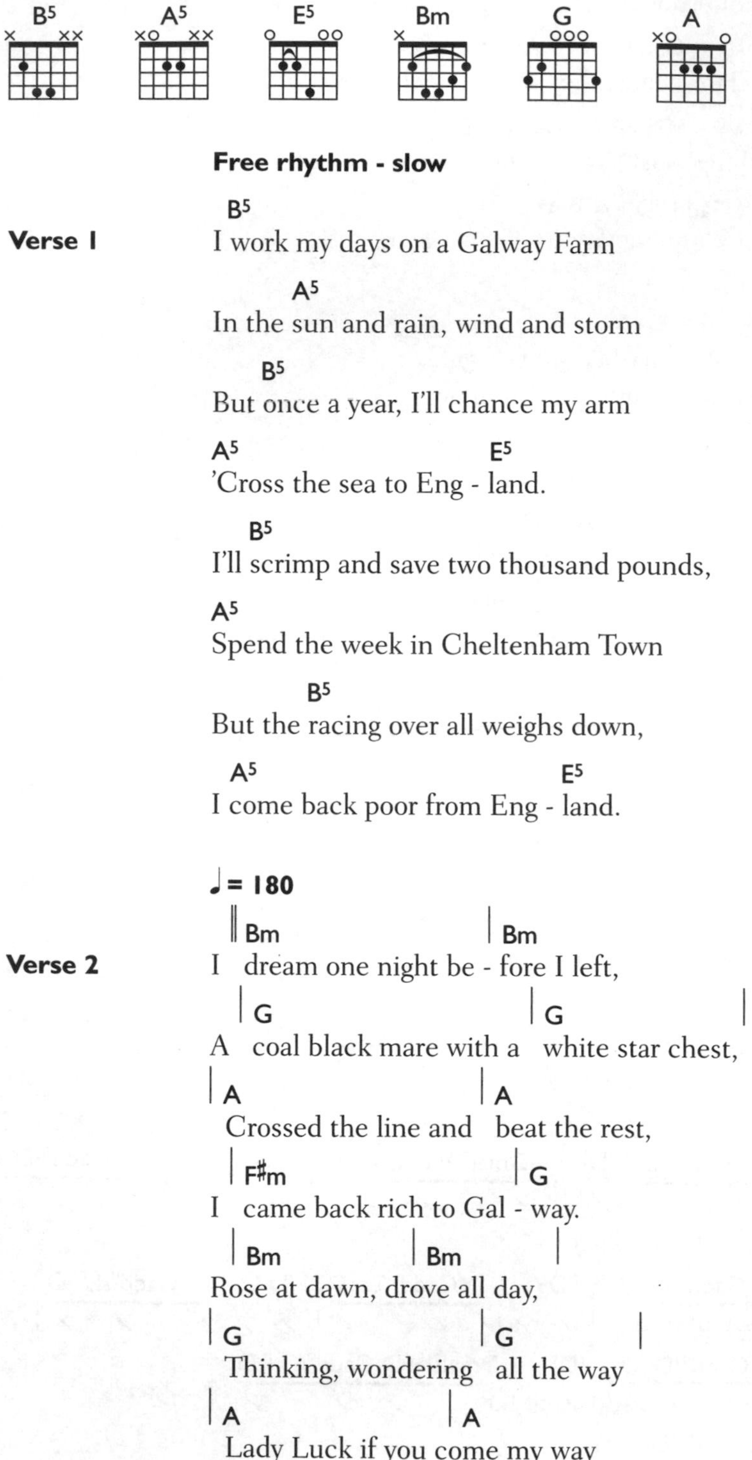

Free rhythm - slow

Verse 1

```
 B5
I work my days on a Galway Farm
         A5
In the sun and rain, wind and storm
     B5
But once a year, I'll chance my arm
A5                 E5
'Cross the sea to Eng - land.
     B5
I'll scrimp and save two thousand pounds,
A5
Spend the week in Cheltenham Town
            B5
But the racing over all weighs down,
 A5                       E5
I come back poor from Eng - land.
```

♩= 180

Verse 2

```
 ‖ Bm                | Bm
I  dream one night be - fore I left,
  | G                | G               |
A   coal black mare with a   white star chest,
| A                | A
  Crossed the line and   beat the rest,
 | F#m             | G
I  came back rich to Gal - way.
 | Bm          | Bm    |
Rose at dawn, drove all day,
| G                | G         |
  Thinking, wondering  all the way
| A               | A
  Lady Luck if you come my way
```

| F♯m | E5 |
To steal away my morning.

cont.

Violin Link 1

Bm Bm A A E5
Bm Bm A E5

Verse 3

‖ Bm | Bm |
And when I got to Chel - tenham Town,
| A | A
Irish faces all around,
| Bm | Bm |
No bed, no mattress to be found,
| A | E5 |
I slept on the hill - side.
| Bm | Bm |
Spent three days at the viewing ring,
| A | A |
Saw the horses they let in,
| Bm | Bm
Just when I was giving in
| A | E5 | E5
I stood and stared in wonder.

Verse 4

‖ Bm | Bm
With stamp - ing hooves and steaming breath,
| G | G
A coal black mare, with a white star chest,
| A | A |
I ran my finger down the list,
| F♯m | G |
Matched the name and num - ber.
| Bm | Bm
Lady Luck had come half way,
| G | G |
The horse's name was Gal - way Bay,
| A | A
Twenty-to-one the odds that day
| F♯m | E5 ‖
I went to make my wager.

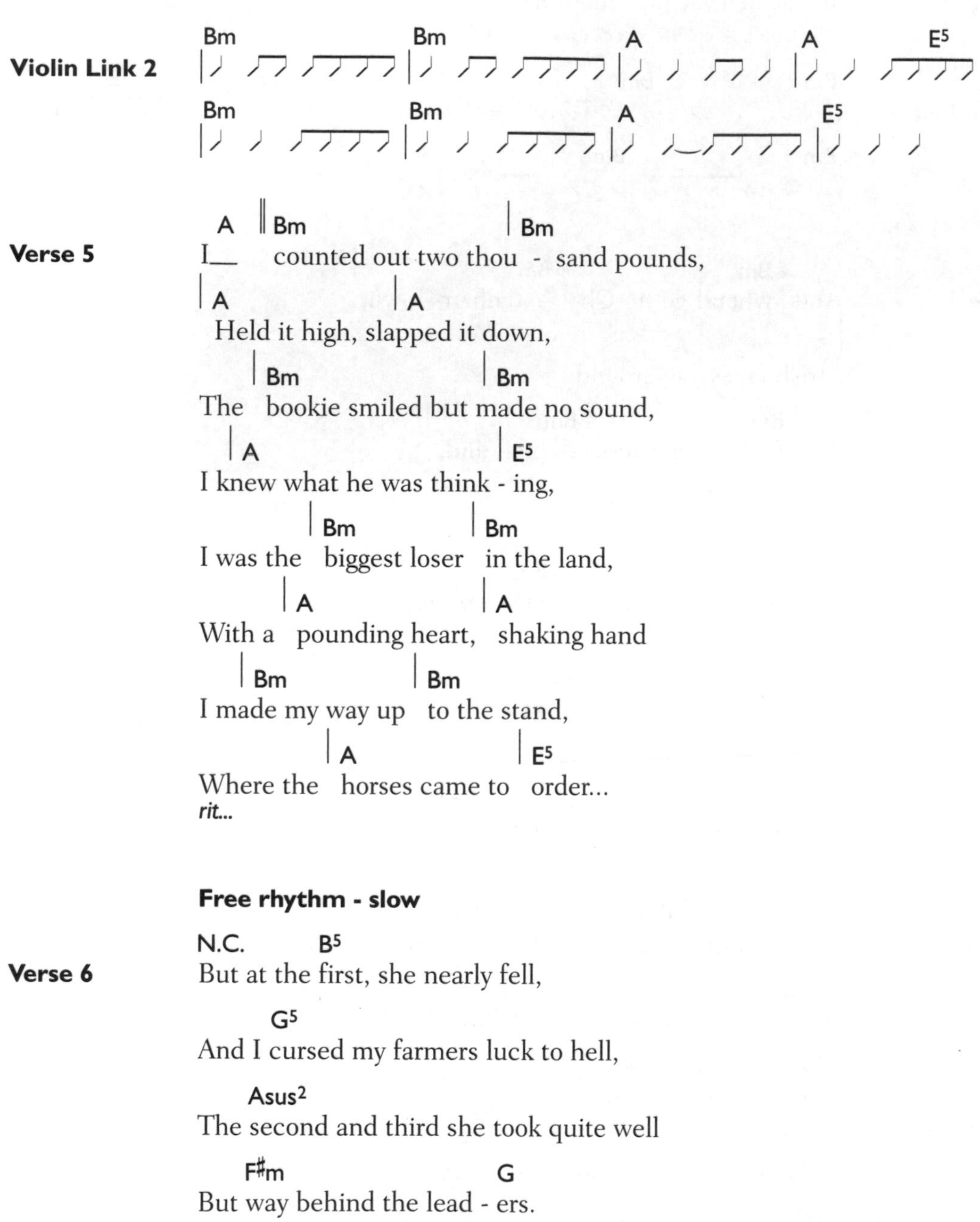
Violin Link 2
Bm Bm A A E5
Bm Bm A E5
Verse 5
A Bm Bm
I__ counted out two thou - sand pounds,
A A
Held it high, slapped it down,
Bm Bm
The bookie smiled but made no sound,
A E5
I knew what he was think - ing,
Bm Bm
I was the biggest loser in the land,
A A
With a pounding heart, shaking hand
Bm Bm
I made my way up to the stand,
A E5
Where the horses came to order...
rit...
Free rhythm - slow
N.C. B5
Verse 6
But at the first, she nearly fell,
G5
And I cursed my farmers luck to hell,
Asus2
The second and third she took quite well
F#m G
But way behind the lead - ers.

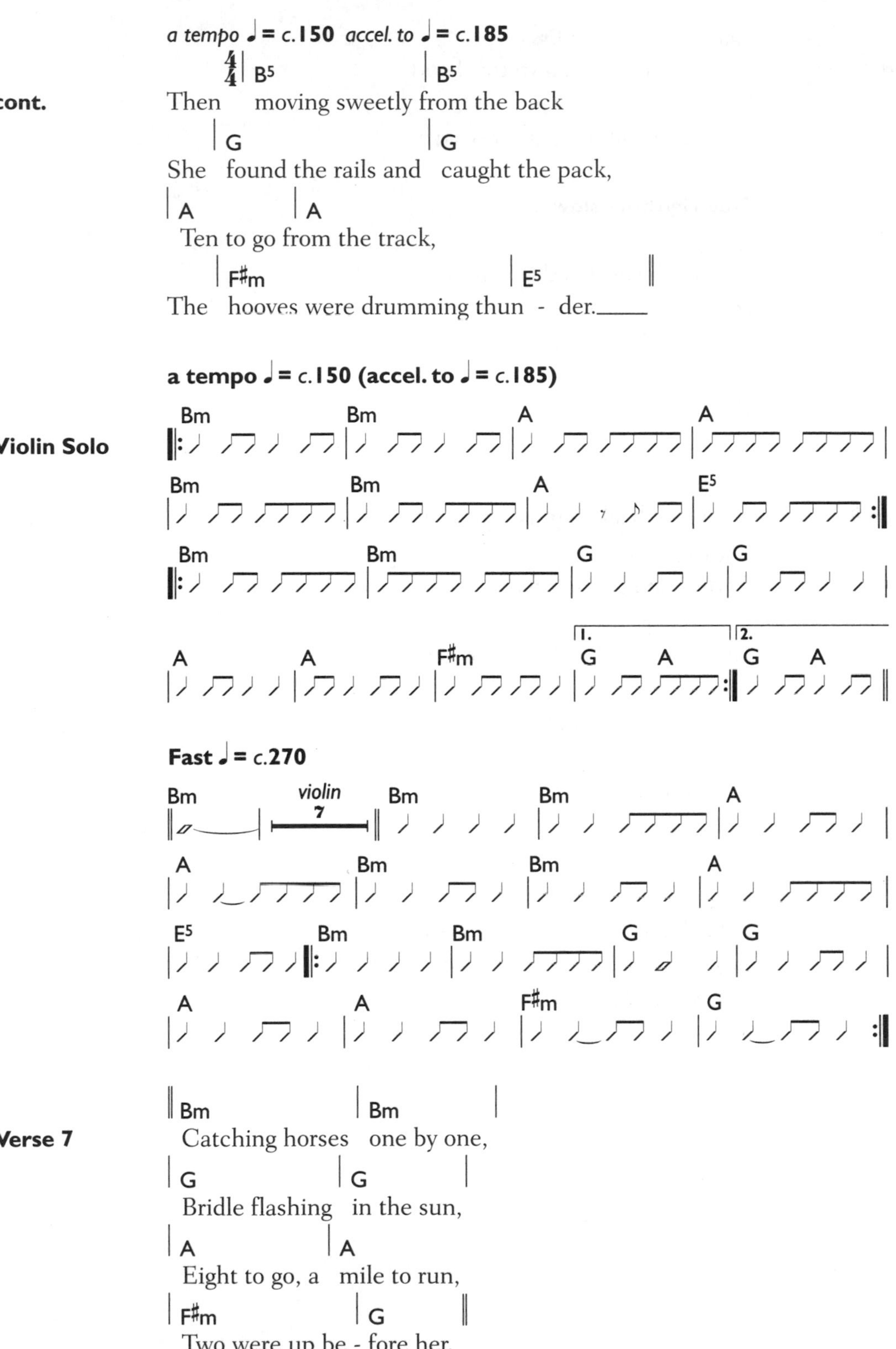
a tempo ♩= c.150 accel. to ♩= c.185
cont.
B5 B5
Then moving sweetly from the back
G G
She found the rails and caught the pack,
A A
Ten to go from the track,
F#m E5
The hooves were drumming thun - der.
a tempo ♩= c.150 (accel. to ♩= c.185)
Violin Solo
Bm Bm A A
Bm Bm A E5
Bm Bm G G
A A F#m 1. G A 2. G A
Fast ♩= c.270
Bm violin 7 Bm Bm A
A Bm Bm A
E5 Bm Bm G G
A A F#m G
Verse 7
Bm Bm
Catching horses one by one,
G G
Bridle flashing in the sun,
A A
Eight to go, a mile to run,
F#m G
Two were up be - fore her.

cont.

```
| Bm                | Bm          |
  On the straight, down this bend
| G                 | G           |
  Left one and the last for dead
```

Free rhythm - slow

```
A
Caught the next and by a head
F#m                 N.C. E5
She came home the winner,

Oh the winner.
```

Verse 8

```
     B5
So I came back to my Galway farm
   Asus2
A wiser and a richer man,
            B5
Never a - gain I'll chance my arm
    A5                      E5
A - cross the sea to Eng - land.
```

a tempo ♩ = 190

```
     || Bm               | Bm
'Cos   Lady Luck was    mine that day
  | G                | G
I   held her close, I   went my way,
  | A
I   raised a glass to Galway Bay
             | F#m    N.C.         | N.C.    E5  |
And the   dreams of a Galway    farmer,
| Bm    | Bm    | G      | G      | A     | A   F#m |
                  I've   won,       I've  won!  rit.
```

Slower

```
| Bm  A  | E5  Bm  | Bm     ||
Oh________    yeah!______
```

GAME OF ALL FOURS

Traditional

Arranged by Kate Rusby

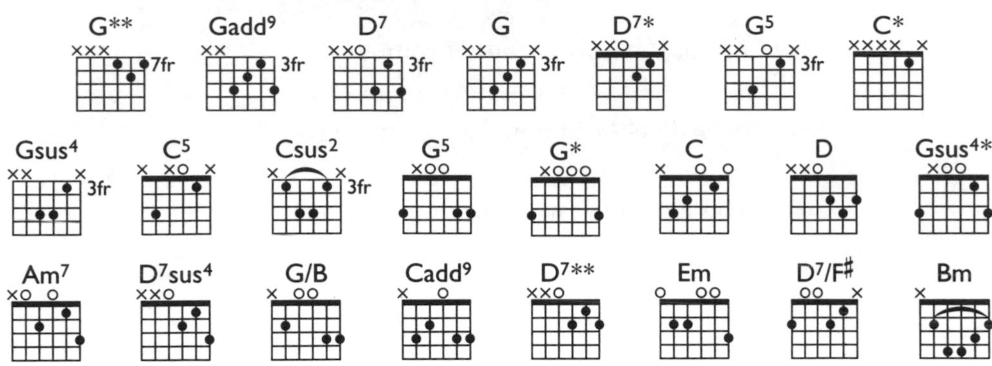

♪ = 192

Intro

6/8 | G** | G** | G** | G** |

| Gadd9 D7* | Gadd9 D7* | Gadd9 D7* | Gadd9 D7* |

Verse 1

```
‖ G                        | D7*
As  I was a walking one  midsummer's morning,
 | G5                           9/8 | C*       D7
To  hear the birds whistle and the  nightingale play,
 6/8 | G                   | G         Gsus4
Was   there that I met a  beautiful maiden,
 9/8 | G      Gsus4      D7*       6/8 | G5  Gsus4 ‖
As I__ was a walking a - long the high - way.
```

Verse 2

```
| G                          | D7
 Where are you going my   fair pretty lady,
| G                     9/8 | C5       D7
 Where are you going so   early this morn?
 6/8 | G                    | G5      Gsus4
She   answered, kind sir, to  visit my neighbours,
 9/8 | G                C5       D7      6/8 | Gadd9  D7
I'm   going down to Lin - coln the place I was   born.
```

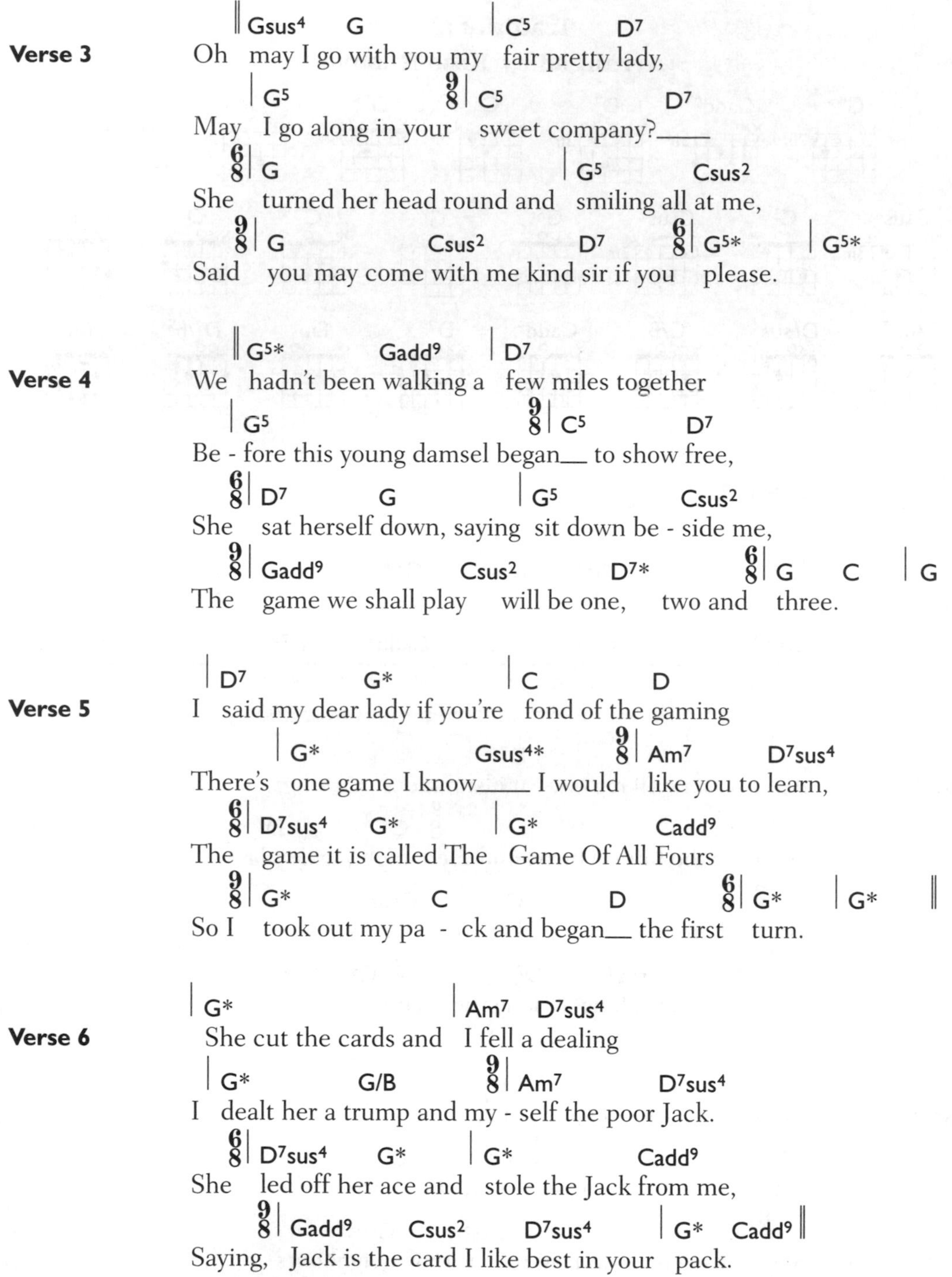

Verse 3

‖ Gsus4 G | C5 D7
Oh may I go with you my fair pretty lady,
| G5 9/8 | C5 D7
May I go along in your sweet company?___
6/8 | G | G5 Csus2
She turned her head round and smiling all at me,
9/8 | G Csus2 D7 6/8 | G5* | G5*
Said you may come with me kind sir if you please.

Verse 4

‖ G5* Gadd9 | D7
We hadn't been walking a few miles together
| G5 9/8 | C5 D7
Be - fore this young damsel began__ to show free,
6/8 | D7 G | G5 Csus2
She sat herself down, saying sit down be - side me,
9/8 | Gadd9 Csus2 D7* 6/8 | G C | G D7 ‖
The game we shall play will be one, two and three.

Verse 5

| D7 G* | C D
I said my dear lady if you're fond of the gaming
| G* Gsus4* 9/8 | Am7 D7sus4
There's one game I know____ I would like you to learn,
6/8 | D7sus4 G* | G* Cadd9
The game it is called The Game Of All Fours
9/8 | G* C D 6/8 | G* | G* ‖
So I took out my pa - ck and began__ the first turn.

Verse 6

| G* | Am7 D7sus4
She cut the cards and I fell a dealing
| G* G/B 9/8 | Am7 D7sus4
I dealt her a trump and my - self the poor Jack.
6/8 | D7sus4 G* | G* Cadd9
She led off her ace and stole the Jack from me,
9/8 | Gadd9 Csus2 D7sus4 | G* Cadd9 ‖
Saying, Jack is the card I like best in your pack.

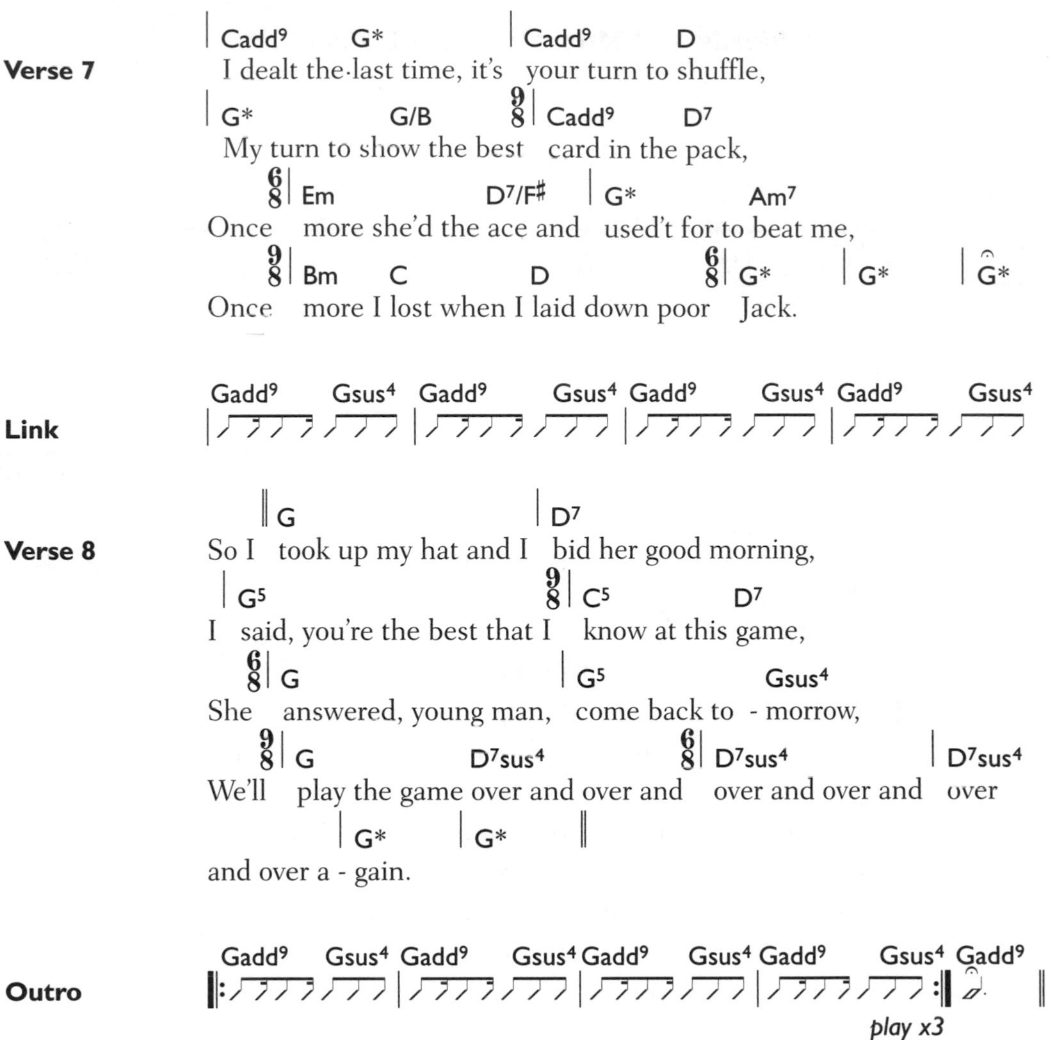
Verse 7
Cadd9 G* Cadd9 D
I dealt the last time, it's your turn to shuffle,
G* G/B 9/8 Cadd9 D7
My turn to show the best card in the pack,
6/8 Em D7/F♯ G* Am7
Once more she'd the ace and used't for to beat me,
9/8 Bm C D 6/8 G* G* G*
Once more I lost when I laid down poor Jack.
Link
Gadd9 Gsus4 Gadd9 Gsus4 Gadd9 Gsus4 Gadd9 Gsus4
Verse 8
G D7
So I took up my hat and I bid her good morning,
G5 9/8 C5 D7
I said, you're the best that I know at this game,
6/8 G G5 Gsus4
She answered, young man, come back to - morrow,
9/8 G D7sus4 6/8 D7sus4 D7sus4
We'll play the game over and over and over and over and over
G* G*
and over a - gain.
Outro
Gadd9 Gsus4 Gadd9 Gsus4 Gadd9 Gsus4 Gadd9 Gsus4 Gadd9
play x3

I WALK THE LINE

Words and Music by John R Cash

F* G* A* B♭ E♭ F C7 A♭

♩= c. 106

Intro

F* G* A* B♭ | E♭ | B♭ | F |
C7 | F | F | F |
F | F ||

I keep a

Verse 1

C7 F
Close watch on this heart of mine, I keep my
C7 F
eyes wide open all the time. I keep the
B♭ F
ends out for the tie that binds, because you're
C7 F
mine, I walk the line.

Link 1

B♭ | B♭ | B♭ | B♭ ||

I find it

Verse 2

F B♭
Very, very easy to be true. I find my-
F B♭
self alone, when each day is through. Yes I'll
E♭ B♭
admit that I'm a fool for you, because you're
F B♭
mine, I walk the line.

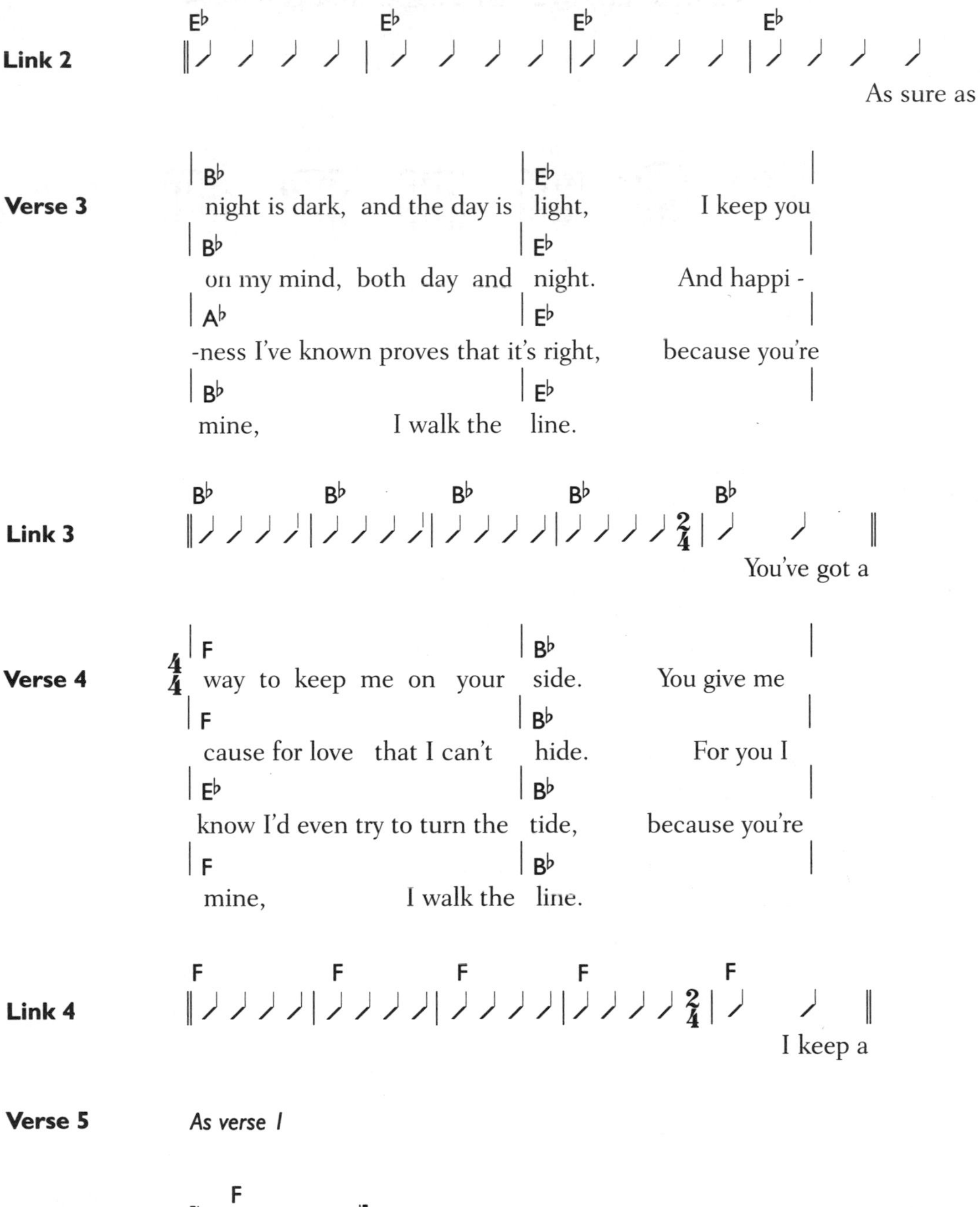

Link 2
E♭ E♭ E♭ E♭
As sure as
Verse 3
B♭ E♭
night is dark, and the day is light, I keep you
B♭ E♭
on my mind, both day and night. And happi -
A♭ E♭
-ness I've known proves that it's right, because you're
B♭ E♭
mine, I walk the line.
Link 3
B♭ B♭ B♭ B♭ B♭
2/4
You've got a
Verse 4
4/4
F B♭
way to keep me on your side. You give me
F B♭
cause for love that I can't hide. For you I
E♭ B♭
know I'd even try to turn the tide, because you're
F B♭
mine, I walk the line.
Link 4
F F F F F
2/4
I keep a
Verse 5
As verse 1
Outro
F
repeat to fade

IF I HAD A HAMMER

Words and Music by Peter Seeger and Lee Hays

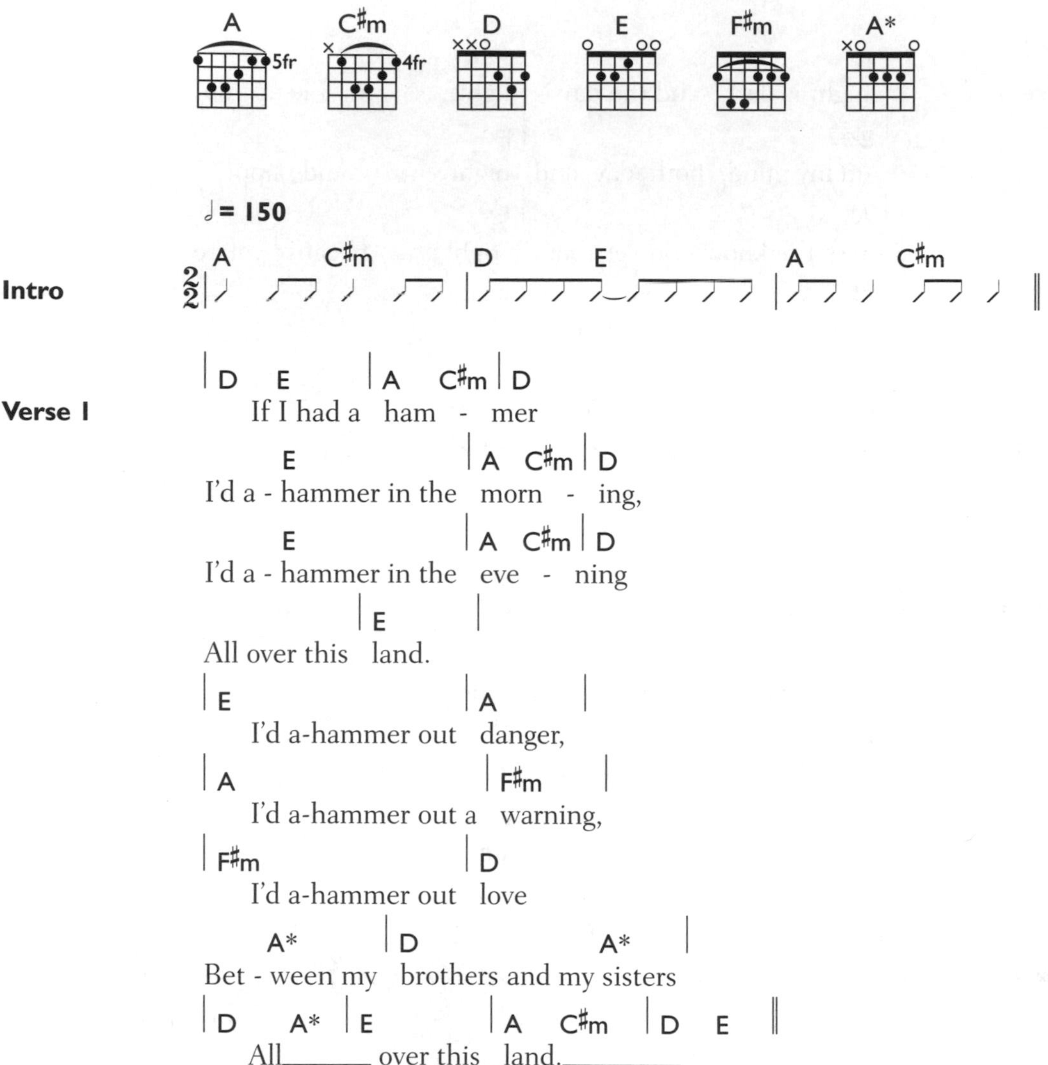

A C#m D E F#m A*
5fr
4fr
♩= 150
Intro
A C#m D E A C#m
Verse 1
D E A C#m D
If I had a ham - mer
E A C#m D
I'd a - hammer in the morn - ing,
E A C#m D
I'd a - hammer in the eve - ning
E
All over this land.
E A
I'd a-hammer out danger,
A F#m
I'd a-hammer out a warning,
F#m D
I'd a-hammer out love
A* D A*
Bet - ween my brothers and my sisters
D A* E A C#m D E
All over this land.

Verse 2

```
| A     C#m | D E           | A    C#m   |
   Ooh,___ if I had a   bell,___
| D      E           | A  C#m | D
  I'd a - ring it in the morn  -  ing
       E              | A  C#m | D
I'd a - ring it in the eve     -     ning
                | E        |
All over this   land.
| E               | A        |
   I'd a-ring out   danger,
| A                  | F#m       |
   I'd a-ring out a   warning,
| F#m              | D
   I'd a-ring out   love
    A*          | D              A*        |
Be - tween my   brothers and my sisters
| D    A*  | E         | A    C#m   | D    E   ||
   All_____ over this   land._______
```

Verse 3

```
| A     C#m | D   E       | A    C#m   |
Ooh,_______ if I had a     song,____
| D     E              | A  C#m | D
__ I'd    sing it in the   morn  -  ing,
   E              | A  C#m | D
I'd sing it in the   eve  -  ning
                | E        |
All over this   land.
| E             | A        |
   I'd sing out   danger,
| A                | F#m       |
   I'd sing out a   warning,
| F#m            | D
   I'd sing out   love
    A*          | D              A*       |
Be - tween my   brothers and my sisters
| D    A*  | E         | A    C#m   | D    E   ||
   All_____ over this   land._______
```

| A C♯m | D E | A C♯m | D

Veres 4 Ooh,_______ well I got a ham - mer,

E | A C♯m |
And I got a bell,____

| D E | A C♯m |
And I got a song to sing
(Song to

| D | E |
All over this land.
sing)

| E | A |
It's the hammer of justice,

| A | F♯m |
It's the bell of free - dom,

| F♯m | D
It's a song about love

A* | D A* |
Be - tween my brothers and my sisters

| D A* | E | A C♯m |
All_____ over this land._____

| D E | A |
It's the hammer of justice,

| A | F♯m |
It's the bell of free - dom,

| F♯m | D
It's a song about love

A* | D A* |
Be - tween my brothers and my sisters

| D A* | E | F♯m | E | A | A ||
All_____ over this land._________________

IF I WERE A CARPENTER

Words and Music by Tim Hardin

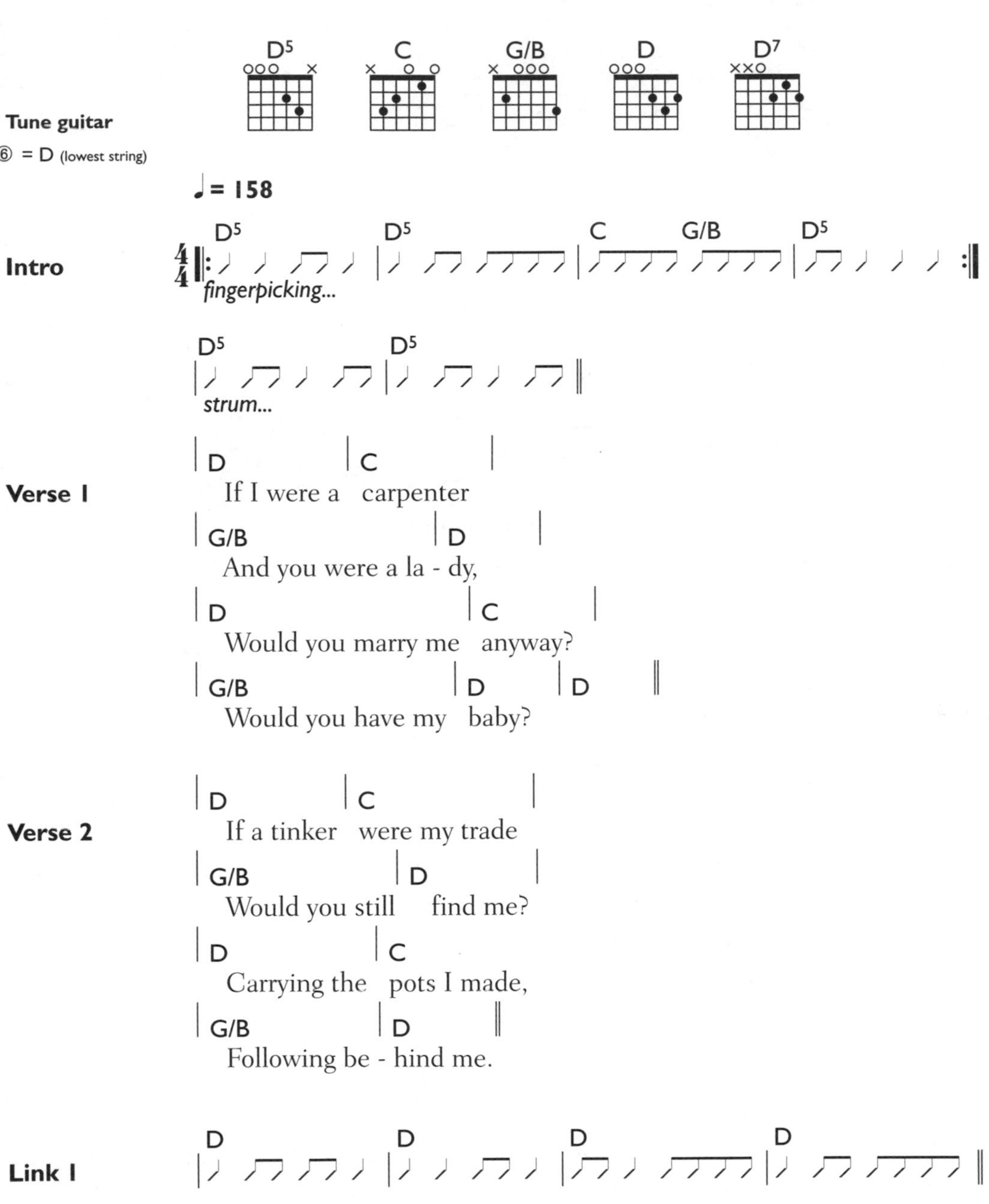
D5 C G/B D D7
Tune guitar
⑥ = D (lowest string)
♩= 158
Intro
D5 D5 C G/B D5
fingerpicking...
D5 D5
strum...
Verse 1
D C
If I were a carpenter
G/B D
And you were a la - dy,
D C
Would you marry me anyway?
G/B D D
Would you have my baby?
Verse 2
D C
If a tinker were my trade
G/B D
Would you still find me?
D C
Carrying the pots I made,
G/B D
Following be - hind me.
Link 1
D D D D

Chorus 1

| C | D |
Save my love for sor - row,
| C | D |
Save my love for lone - ly,
| D | C |
I've given you my tomorrow,
| G/B | D | D ||
Love me only.

Link 2

| D / / ⁄⁄ / | D / / ⁄⁄ / | D / / ⁄⁄ / | D / / ⁄⁄ / ||

Verse 3

| D | C |
If I work my hands in wood,
| G/B | D
Would you still love me?
| D | C |
You answer me quick: "Tim I could,
| G/B | D | D | D ||
I'll put you above me."

Verse 4

| D | C |
If I were a mil - ler,
| G/B | D |
At a mill wheel grinding,
| D | C |
Would you miss your coloured blouse,
| G/B | D | D | D | D ||
Soft shoes a-shining.

Chorus 2

| C | D |
Save my love through loneliness,
| C | D |
Save my love for sorrow,
| D | C |
I've given you my only-ness,
| G/B | D ||
Give me your tomorrow.

Instrumental

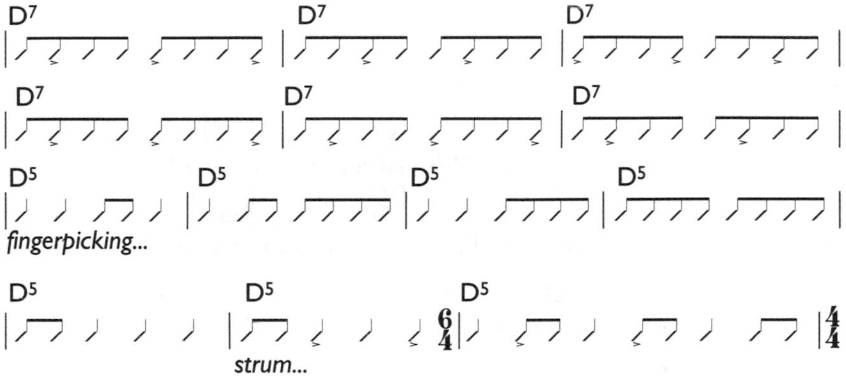

D7	D7	D7
D7	D7	D7
D5	D5	D5	D5
fingerpicking...

| D5 | D5 6/4 | D5 4/4 |
strum...

Verse 5

| D | C |
If I were a carpenter
| G/B | D |
And you were a la - dy,
| D | C |
Would you marry me anyway?
| G/B | D | D ||
Would you have my baby?

Outro

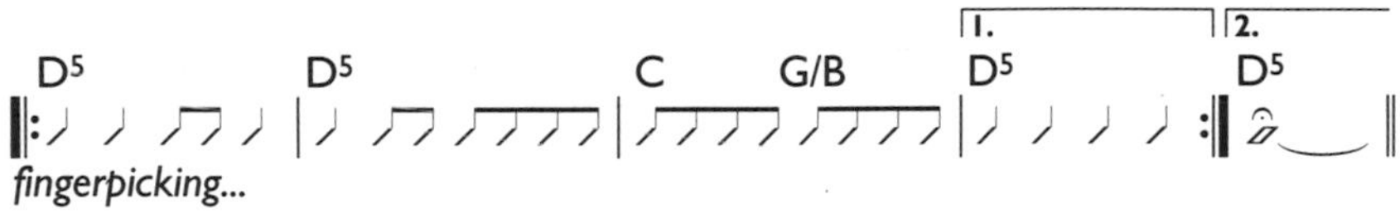

|: D5 | D5 | C G/B | 1. D5 :| 2. D5 ||
fingerpicking...

THE IRISH ROVER

Words and Music Traditional
Arranged by Joseph Crofts

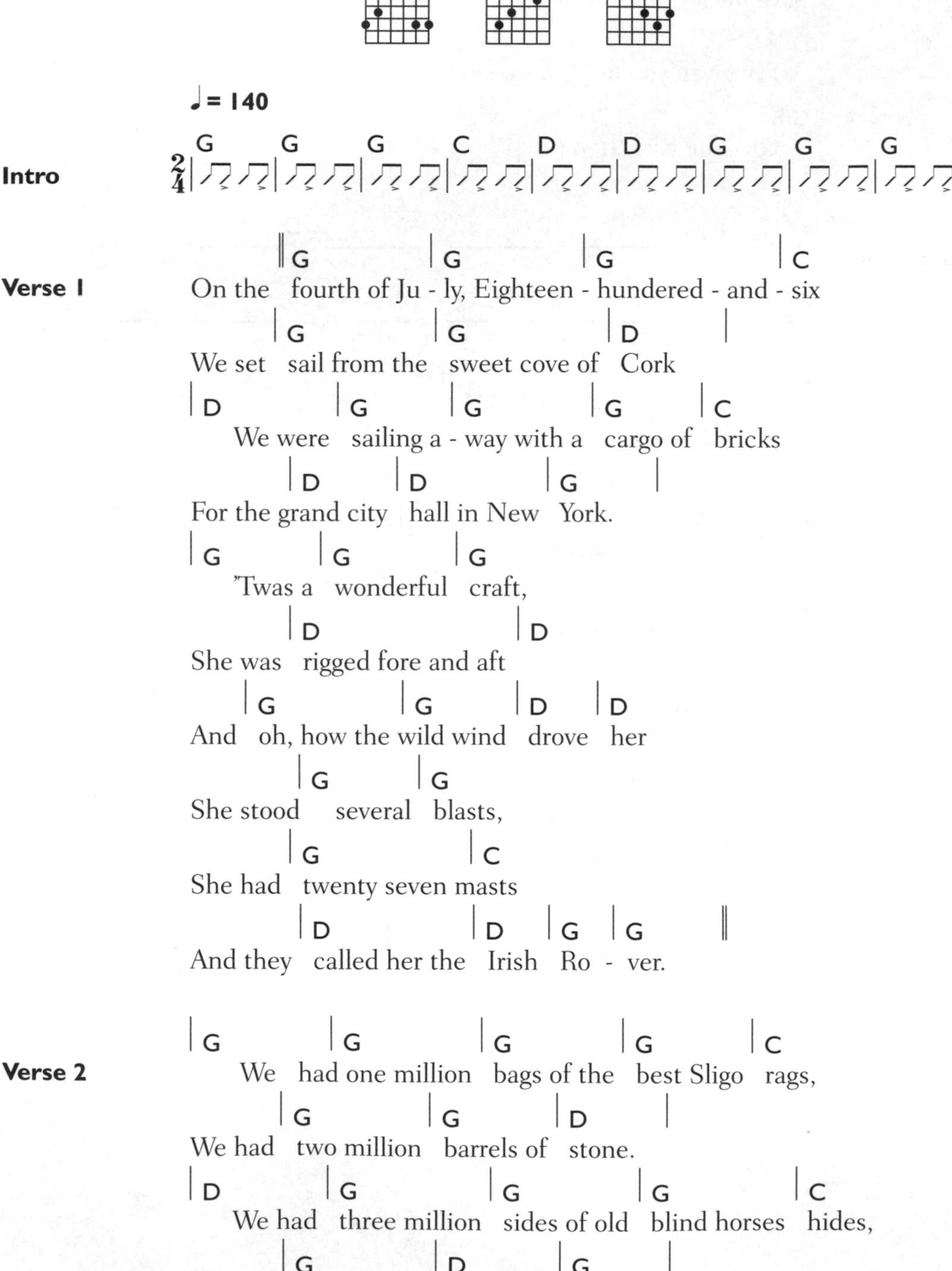

cont.

| G | G | G |
We had five million hogs,
| D | D |
Six million dogs,
| G | G | D | D
Seven million barrels of por - ter
| G | G | G | C
We had eight million bails of old nanny-goats' tails
| G | G | D | G ‖
In the hold of the Irish Ro - ver

Verse 3

| G | G | G
There was awl Mickey Coote
| G | C
Who played hard on his flute
| G | G | D |
When the la - dies lined up for the set.
| D | G | G
He was tootin' with skill
| G | C
For each sparkling qua - drille
| G | D | G |
Though the dancers were fluther'd and bet.
| G | G | G
With his smart witty talk
| D | D
He was cock of the walk
| G | G | D | D
And he rolled the dames under and ov - er,
| G | G
They all knew at a glance
| G | C
When he took up his stance
| D | D | G | G | G ‖
That he sailed in the Irish Ro - ver.

Instrumental

G	G	G	C	G	G	D	D
G	G	G	C	G	D	G	G
G	G	D	D	G	G	D	D
G	G	G	C	D	D	G	G	

Verse 4

[G] There was [G] Barney Mc - [G] Gee
From the [G] banks of the [C] Lee
There was [G] Hogan from [G] County Ty - [D] rone |
[D] There was [G] Johnny Mc - [G] Gurk
Who was [G] scared stiff of [C] work
And a [G] man from West - [D] meath called Ma - [G] lone. |
[G] There was [G] Slugger O' - [G] Toole
Who was [D] drunk as a [D] rule
And [G] fighting Bill [G] Treacy from [D] Do - [D] ver
And [G] your man, Mick Mac - [G] Cann,
From the [G] banks of the [C] Bann
Was the [G] skipper of the [G] Irish [D] Ro - [G] ver. ||

Verse 5

```
|G        |G          |G
   We had  sailed seven  years
                  |G        |C
When the mea - sles broke  out
       |G         |G         |D       |
And the  ship lost it's  way in  the fog.
|D         |G         |G
   And that  whale of a  crew
      |G           |C
Was re - duced down to  two,
    |G          |D          |G       |
Just  myself and the  captain's old  dog.
|G          |G          |G
   Then the  ship struck a  rock,
   |D         |D
Oh  Lord! What a  shock
N.C. |G          |G          |D    |D(fermata)
  The  bulkhead was  turned right  ov - er...
```

Free rhythm, slow

```
      G
Turned nine times around
                     C(fermata)
And the poor old dog was drowned
```

a tempo

```
       |G        |G   |D    |G    |G   ||
And the  last of the  Irish  Ro -  ver.
```

Outro

```
 G    G    G    C    G    G    D    D
|/ / |/ / |/ / |/ / |/ / |/ / |/ / |/ / |
 G    G    G    C    G    D    G    G
|/ / |/ / |/ / |/ / |/ / |/ / |/ / |/ / |
 G    G    D    D    G    G    D    D
|/ / |/ / |/ / |/ / |/ / |/ / |/ / |/ / |
 G    G    G    C    D    D    G    G
|/ / |/ / |/ / |/ / |/ / |/ / |/ / |(fermata) ||
                                rit.
```

I'M GONNA BE (500 MILES)

Words and Music by Charles Reid and Craig Reid

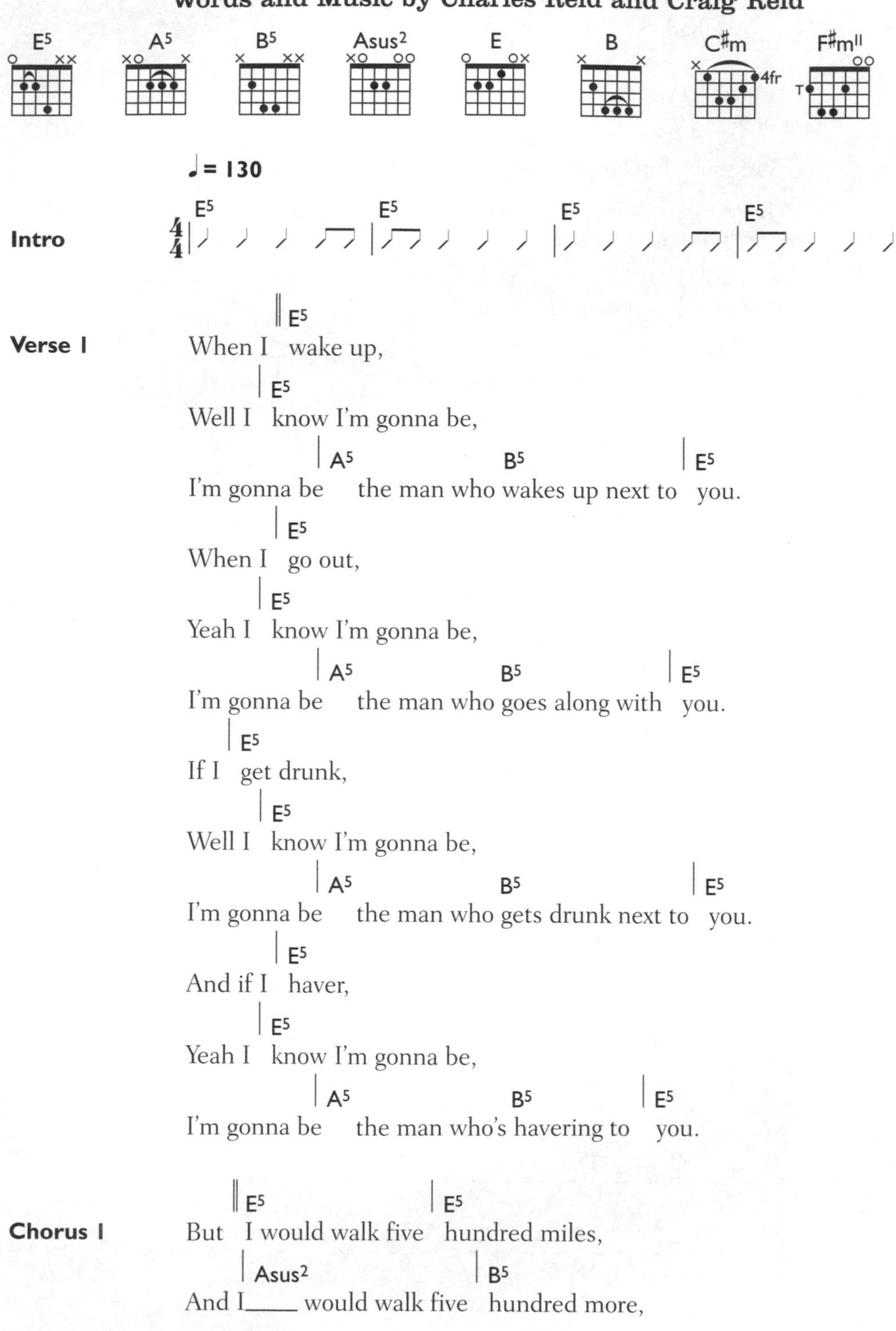
E5 A5 B5 Asus2 E B C#m F#m11 B9sus4
4fr
♩= 130
Intro
E5 E5 E5 E5
Verse 1
E5
When I wake up,
E5
Well I know I'm gonna be,
A5 B5 E5
I'm gonna be the man who wakes up next to you.
E5
When I go out,
E5
Yeah I know I'm gonna be,
A5 B5 E5
I'm gonna be the man who goes along with you.
E5
If I get drunk,
E5
Well I know I'm gonna be,
A5 B5 E5
I'm gonna be the man who gets drunk next to you.
E5
And if I haver,
E5
Yeah I know I'm gonna be,
A5 B5 E5
I'm gonna be the man who's havering to you.
Chorus 1
E5 E5
But I would walk five hundred miles,
Asus2 B5
And I____ would walk five hundred more,

cont.

| E5 | E5 | Asus2
Just to be the man who walked that thousand miles
| B5
To fall down at your door.

Verse 2

|| E5
When I'm working,
| E5
Yes I know I'm gonna be,
| A5 B5 | E5
I'm gonna be the man who's working hard for you.
| E5
And when the money
| E5
Comes in for the work I do
| A5 B5 | E5
I'll pass almost every penny on to you.
| E5
When I come home, *(when I come home),*
| E5
Oh I know I'm gonna be,
| A5 B5 | E5
I'm gonna be the man who comes back home to you.
| E5
And if I grow old,
| E5
Well I know I'm gonna be,
| A5 B5 | E5
I'm gonna be the man who's growing old with you.

Chorus 2

As Chorus 1

Bridge 1

|| E | E
Da-da-da - da, da-da-da-da, da-da-da - da, da-da-da-da,
| Asus2 B | E
Da-da dun-da-da-dun-da-da - dun-da-da da-da - da.
| E | E
Da-da-da - da, da-da-da-da, da-da-da - da, da-da-da-da,
| Asus2 B | E ||
Da-da dun-da-da-dun-da-da - dun-da-da da-da - da.

Link

E^5 E^5
| / / / / / | / / / / /

Verse 3

‖ E^5
When I'm lonely,
| E^5
Well I know I'm gonna be,
| A^5 B^5 | E^5
I'm gonna be the man who's lonely without you.
| E^5
And when I'm dreaming,
| E^5
Well I know I'm gonna dream,
| A^5 | B^5 | E^5
I'm gonna dream about the time when I'm with you.
| E^5
When I go out, *(when I go out)*
| E^5
Well I know I'm gonna be,
| A^5 B^5 | E^5
I'm gonna be the man who goes along with you.
| E^5
And when I come home, *(when I come home),*
| E^5
Yes I know I'm gonna be,
| A^5 B^5 | C♯m
I'm gonna be the man who comes back home with you
$\frac{2}{4}$| F♯m^{11} $\frac{4}{4}$| B^{9}sus^4 | E^5 | E^5
I'm gonna be the man who's coming home with you.

Chorus 3 *As Chorus 1*

Bridge 2 ‖: *As Bridge 1* :‖

Chorus 4

‖ E
And I would walk five hundred miles,
| Asus^2 B
And I would walk five hundred more,
| E | Asus^2
Just to be the man who walked a thousand miles
B | E ‖
To fall down at your door.____

LIGHT FLIGHT

Words and Music by Bert Jansch, John Renbourn, Danny Thompson, Terry Cox and Jacqui McShee

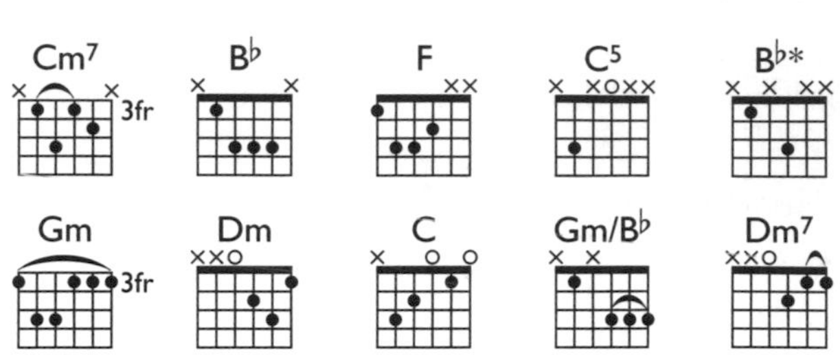

♩ = 180

Cm7 Bb F Cm7
6/4 ‖: | | | :‖
riffs plucked w/fingers

Cm7 (C) (Bb) (C) (Bb) (F) | C5 Bb* | C5 Bb* F
5/4 7/4 5/4 7/4 ‖
(double bass)

Verse 1

5/4 C5 Bb* 7/4 C5 Bb* F 5/4 C5
"Let's get a - way" you say, "find a better place,___
Bb* 7/4 C5 Bb* F
Miles and miles a - way from the city's race."
5/4 Gm Dm 7/4 Gm Dm
Look around for someone lying in the sunshine
C 5/4 Dm C 7/4 Dm C Gm/Bb
Marking time, hear the sighs, close your eyes…
5/4 C5 Bb* 7/4 C5 Bb* F ‖
Ba da ba do da, da ba da do da da…

Link 1

C5 Bb* C5 Bb* F
5/4 7/4 ‖

Verse 2

5/4 | C5 Bb* 7/4 | C5 Bb* F ||
Stepping from cloud to cloud passing years of light,
5/4 | C5 Bb* 7/4 | C5 Bb* F |
Visit the frosty stars in the backward flight
5/4 | Gm Dm 7/4 | Gm Dm C 5/4 | Dm
Soaring runs of visions, never mind the meaning hidden there,
C 7/4 | Dm C Gm/Bb |
Moving fast, it won't last.
5/4 | C5 Bb* 7/4 | C5 Bb* F ||
Ba da ba do da, da da ba do da da.

Link 2

As Link 1

Verse 3

5/4 | C5 Bb* 7/4 | C5 Bb* F 5/4 | C5
Time passes all too soon, how it rushes by,____
Bb* 7/4 | C5 Bb* F |
Now a thousand moons are a - bout to die
5/4 | Gm Dm 7/4 | Gm Dm
No time to re - flect on what the time was spent on,
C 5/4 | Dm C 7/4 | Dm C Gm/Bb |
Nothing left, far a - way, dreamers fade.
5/4 | C5 Bb* 7/4 | C5 Bb* F ||
Ba da ba do da, da da ba do da da.

Link 3

Cm7 Cm7 Cm7 Cm7
6/4 | / / / /// /// /// | / / / /// /// /// | / /// ///-/// / / | / /// ///-///-/ / ||

Bridge

6/4 | Cm7 | Bb | F | Cm7 |
Strange visions pass me by,
| Gm | Dm | Cm7 | Gm |
Winging sweetly close in - side,
| Cm7 | Bb | F | Cm7 | Cm7 ||
Ov - er the wa - ter.

Instrumental

Cm7 Bb F Cm7

Ah,

Gm Dm7 Cm7

Ah,

Gm7 Cm7 Bb

Ah,

F Cm7 Cm7 (C) (Bb) (C) (Bb) (F)

Ah... (bass)

Verse 4

C5 Bb* C5 Bb* F
Swirling, the waters rise up a - bove my head.

C5 Bb* C5 Bb* F
Gone are the curling mists how they all have fled.

Gm Dm Gm Dm
Look, the door is open, step into the space

C Dm C Dm C Gm/Bb
Pro - vided there, da do da, da do da.

C5 Bb* C5 Bb* F
Ba da ba do da, da da ba do da da.

Outro

C5 Bb* C5 Bb* F

Cm7 Cm7 N.C.

LET IT BLOW

Words and Music by Richard Thompson

Tune lowest string

⑥ = D

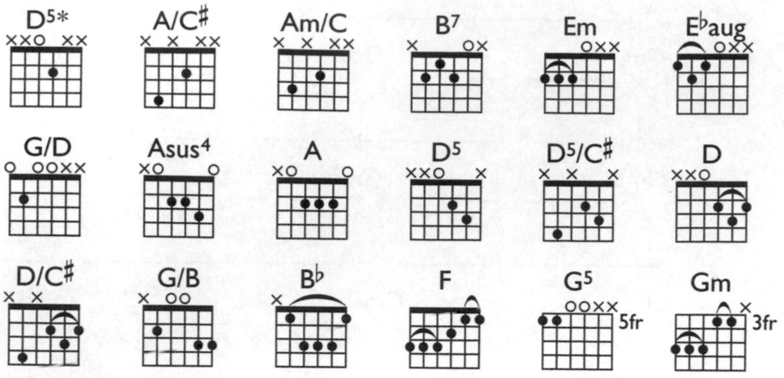

D5* A/C♯ Am/C B7 Em E♭aug

G/D Asus4 A D5 D5/C♯ D

D/C♯ G/B B♭ F G5 5fr Gm 3fr

♩= 140

Verse 1

| D5* | A/C♯

He was a spe - cies on the verge of extinc - tion,

| Am/C | B7

She was an Air New Zealand hos - tess

| Em | E♭aug

They were mys - tically joined, like Rawicz and Landauer

| G/D | Asus4 A

Like Pinky and Perky, like Porgy and Bess.

| D5 | D5/C♯

O he loved the pursuit and the ro - mance

| Am/C | B7

But the de - tails were more of a chore

| Em | E♭aug

When the bride's veil lifted, his mind soon drifted

| G/D | Asus4

At least that's what happened before.

Chorus 1

A ‖ D | D/C♯

Let It Blow, let it snow,

| G/B | A

Let the mer - cury bubble and dive,___

| B♭ | F

Life's little traumas and court - room dramas

| G5 | A | A ‖

Re - mind me I'm glad I'm alive.___

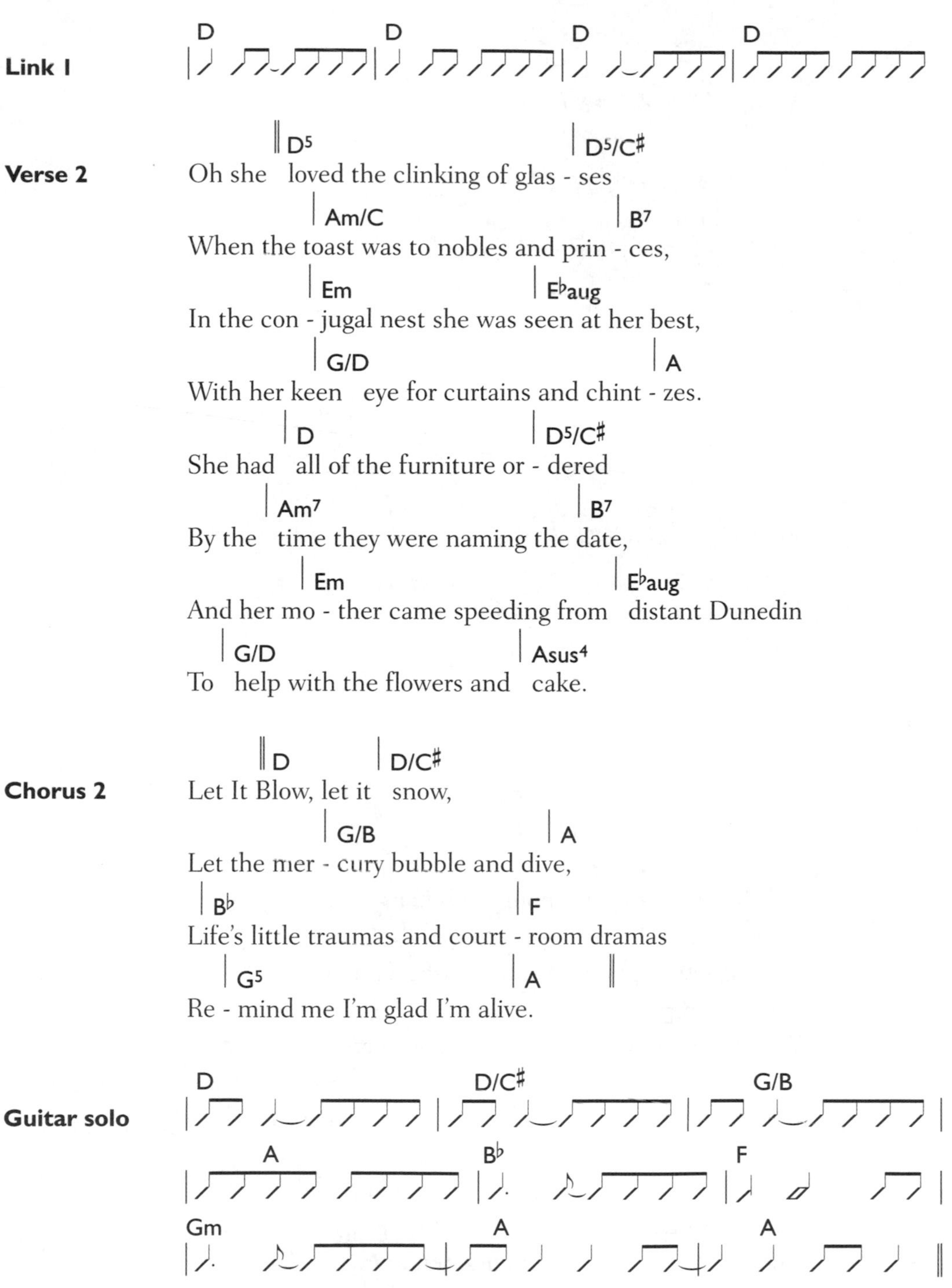
D D D D
Link 1
D5 D5/C#
Verse 2
Oh she loved the clinking of glas - ses
Am/C B7
When the toast was to nobles and prin - ces,
Em E♭aug
In the con - jugal nest she was seen at her best,
G/D A
With her keen eye for curtains and chint - zes.
D D5/C#
She had all of the furniture or - dered
Am7 B7
By the time they were naming the date,
Em E♭aug
And her mo - ther came speeding from distant Dunedin
G/D Asus4
To help with the flowers and cake.
D D/C#
Chorus 2
Let It Blow, let it snow,
G/B A
Let the mer - cury bubble and dive,
B♭ F
Life's little traumas and court - room dramas
G5 A
Re - mind me I'm glad I'm alive.
D D/C# G/B
Guitar solo
A B♭ F
Gm A A

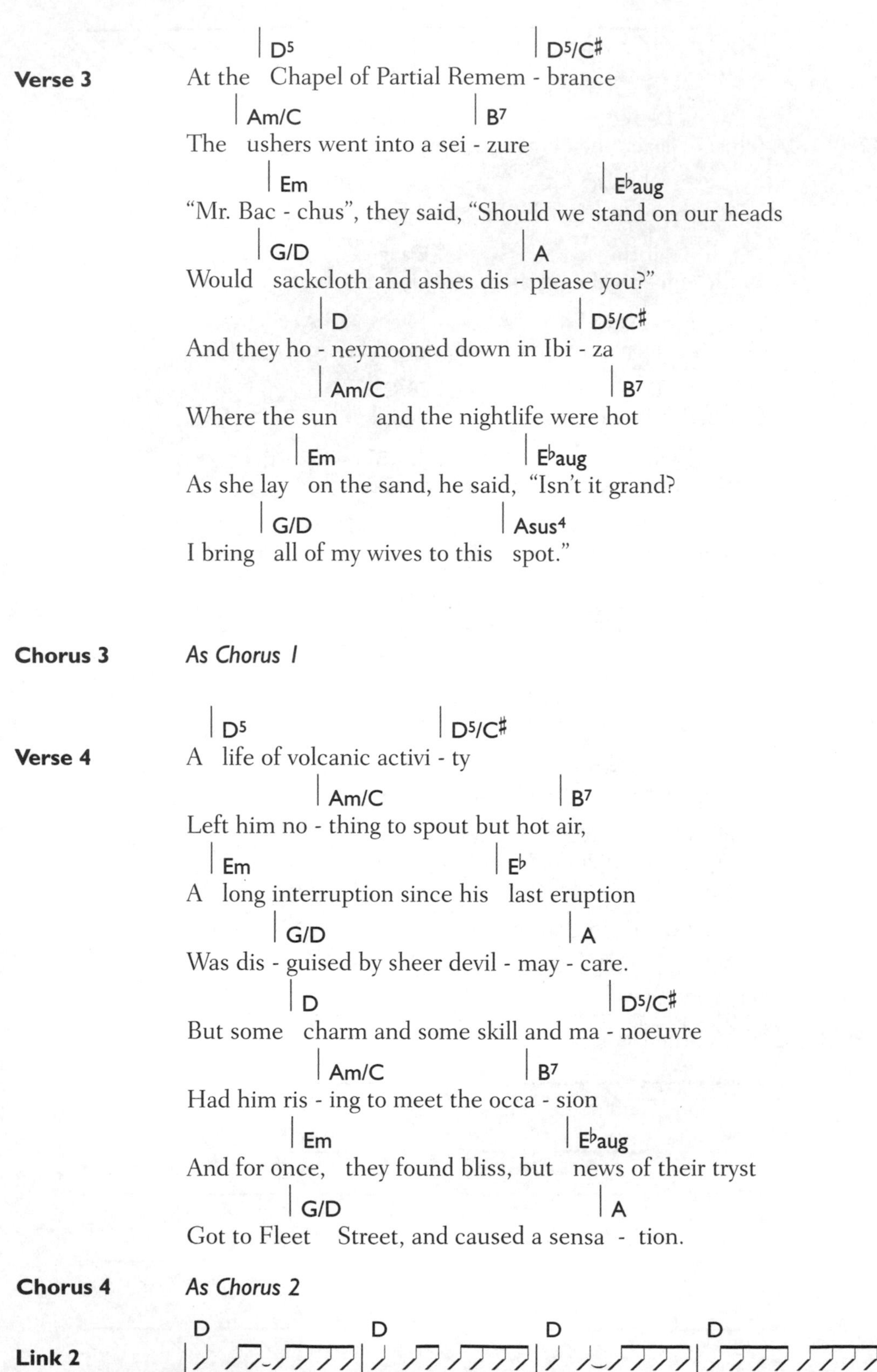

Verse 3

| D5 | D5/C# |
At the Chapel of Partial Remem - brance
| Am/C | B7 |
The ushers went into a sei - zure
| Em | E♭aug |
"Mr. Bac - chus", they said, "Should we stand on our heads
| G/D | A |
Would sackcloth and ashes dis - please you?"
| D | D5/C# |
And they ho - neymooned down in Ibi - za
| Am/C | B7 |
Where the sun and the nightlife were hot
| Em | E♭aug |
As she lay on the sand, he said, "Isn't it grand?
| G/D | Asus4 |
I bring all of my wives to this spot."

Chorus 3 *As Chorus 1*

Verse 4

| D5 | D5/C# |
A life of volcanic activi - ty
| Am/C | B7 |
Left him no - thing to spout but hot air,
| Em | E♭ |
A long interruption since his last eruption
| G/D | A |
Was dis - guised by sheer devil - may - care.
| D | D5/C# |
But some charm and some skill and ma - noeuvre
| Am/C | B7 |
Had him ris - ing to meet the occa - sion
| Em | E♭aug |
And for once, they found bliss, but news of their tryst
| G/D | A |
Got to Fleet Street, and caused a sensa - tion.

Chorus 4 *As Chorus 2*

Link 2

D D D D

Verse 5

```
          ‖ D5*                           | A/C#
And the   Press was baying for blood        now,
    | Am/C                         | B7
They   gave them a week at the most.
          | Em                       | E♭aug
We were   all glad to see it reach   weeks two and three
          | G/D                                | A
But the fourth week, the whole thing was toast.
Asus4     | D5                                  | D5/C#
And the she   dragged her tail back to New Zea  -  land,
    | Am/C                           | B7
With   threats of High Court and re - venge,
               | Em                   | E♭aug
Meanwhile   his eye did stray to the   ample bustier
       | G/D               | A
Of a   novelty dancer from Penge.
```

Chorus 5

```
             ‖ D          | D/C#
Let It Blow, let it        snow,
                  | G/B          | A
Let the mer - cury bubble and dive,
  | B♭                             | F
Life's little traumas and court - room dramas
   | Gm                          | A      | A
Re - mind me I'm glad I'm alive.                Ah,
             | D          | D/C#
Let It Blow, let it        snow,
                  | G/B          | A
Let the mer - cury bubble and dive,
  | B♭                             | F
Life's little traumas and court - room dramas
   | Gm                          | A      | A      ‖
Re - mind me I'm glad I'm alive.__________
```

Outro

```
    D                      D/C#                    G/B
𝄆 / /‿/ / / /           | / / /‿/ / / /           | / / / / / / / /        |
    A                      B♭                      F
| / / / / / / / /       | / / /‿/ / / /           | / /‿/ / / /            |
    G5                     A                       A
| / / / / / / / /       | / / / / / /‿            / / / / / / / /         𝄇
```

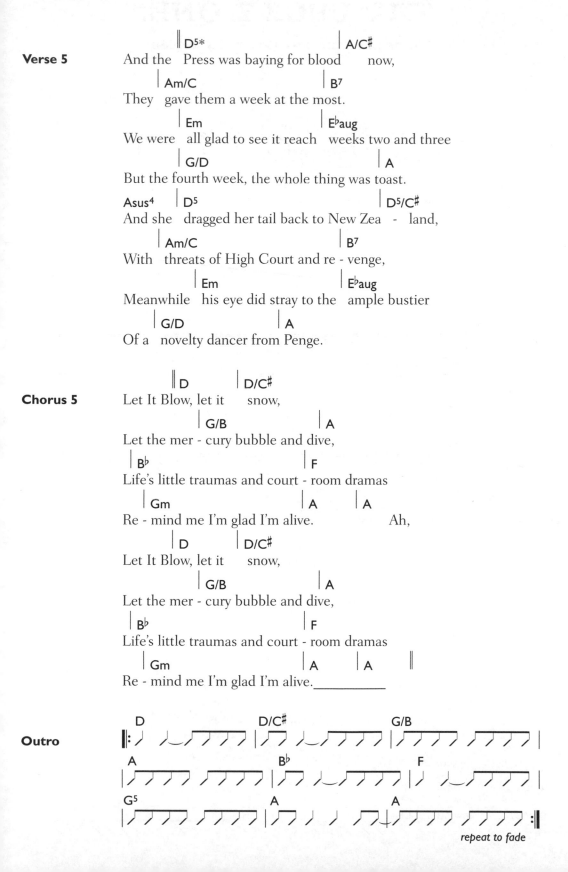

repeat to fade

THE LUCKY ONE

Words and Music by Robert Castleman

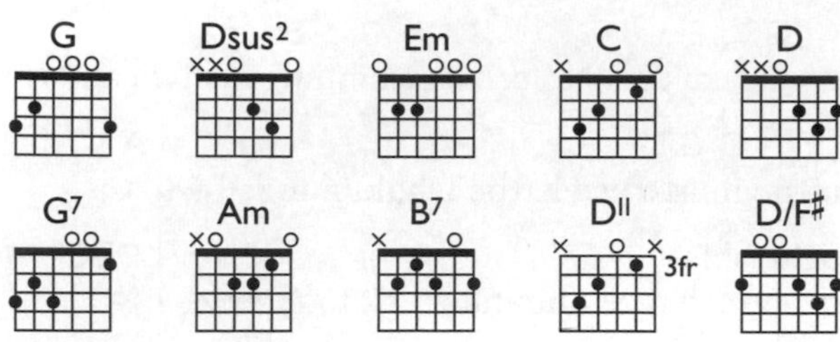

Capo 3rd Fret

♩ = 84

Intro

4/4 | G | Dsus2 |
Em	C
G	Dsus2	
C	G

Verse 1

G
You're the lucky one so I've been told,

D
As free as the wind blowing down the road,

G
Loved by many, hated by none,

C
I'd say you were lucky 'cos I know what you've done,

G
No care in the world, not a worry in sight,

D
Everything's gonna be alright

C G
'Cos you're the lucky one.

Verse 2

```
            ‖G
You're the   lucky one, always having fun,
  |D
A  Jack of all trades, a master of none,
    |G                         G7
You  look at the world with a smiling eye
       |C                                  |
And laugh at the devil as his train rolls by,
|G                                         |
 Give you a song, and a one night stand,
|D
   You'll be looking at a happy man
                |C         |G
'Cos you're the  lucky one.
```

Chorus 1

```
              ‖Am
Well you're    blessed I guess
                 |D
By never know - ing which road you're choosin'
                |Am
To you the next   best thing
                  2/4|D       B7         4/4|Em
To playin' and win  -  ning is playin' and los  -  ing.
```

Verse 3

```
            ‖G
You're the   lucky one, I know that now
     |D
Don't  ask you why, when, where, or how
    |G7
You  look at the world with a smilin' eye
     |C                                   |
And laugh at the devil as his train goes by
|G                                      |
 Give you a song and a one night stand
|D
   And you'll be looking at a happy man
                |C         |G          ‖
'Cos you're the  lucky one.
```

Instrumental
G
D11
G
G7
C
G
Dsus2
C
G
Chorus 2
As Chorus 1
Verse 4
G
You're the lucky one I know that now
D/F#
Don't ask you why, when, where, or how
G
G7
No matter where you're at, it's where you'll be
C
You can bet your luck won't follow me,
G
Just give you a song and a one night stand
D
You'll be looking at a happy man
C
G
'Cos you're the lucky one.
Outro
G
D
Em
C
G
D
C
G

PART OF THE UNION

Words and Music by Richard Hudson and John Ford

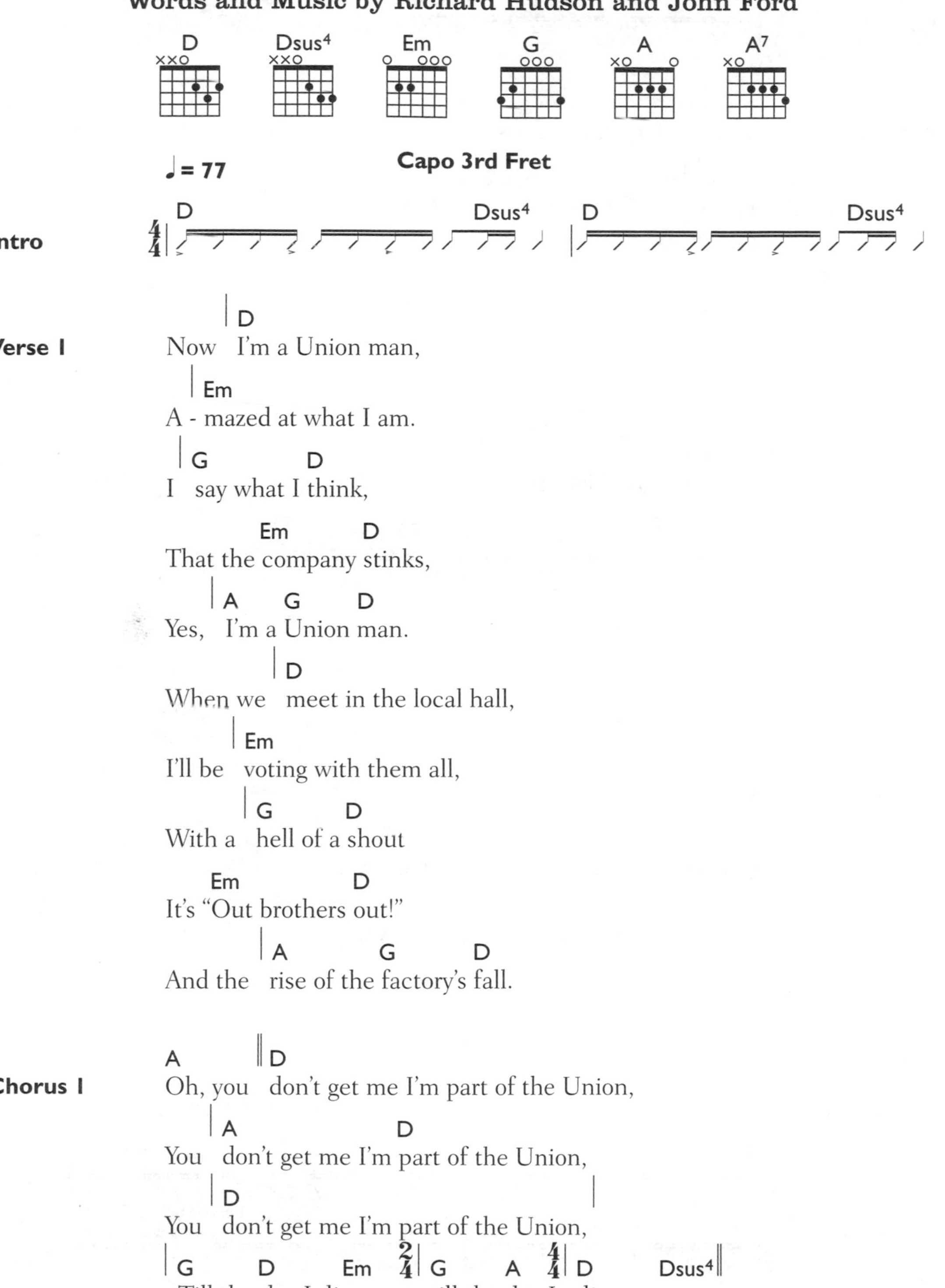
D
Dsus4
Em
G
A
A7
♩ = 77
Capo 3rd Fret
Intro
D
Dsus4
D
Dsus4
Verse 1
D
Now I'm a Union man,
Em
A - mazed at what I am.
G D
I say what I think,
Em D
That the company stinks,
A G D
Yes, I'm a Union man.
D
When we meet in the local hall,
Em
I'll be voting with them all,
G D
With a hell of a shout
Em D
It's "Out brothers out!"
A G D
And the rise of the factory's fall.
Chorus 1
A D
Oh, you don't get me I'm part of the Union,
A D
You don't get me I'm part of the Union,
D
You don't get me I'm part of the Union,
G D Em G A D Dsus4
Till the day I die, till the day I die.

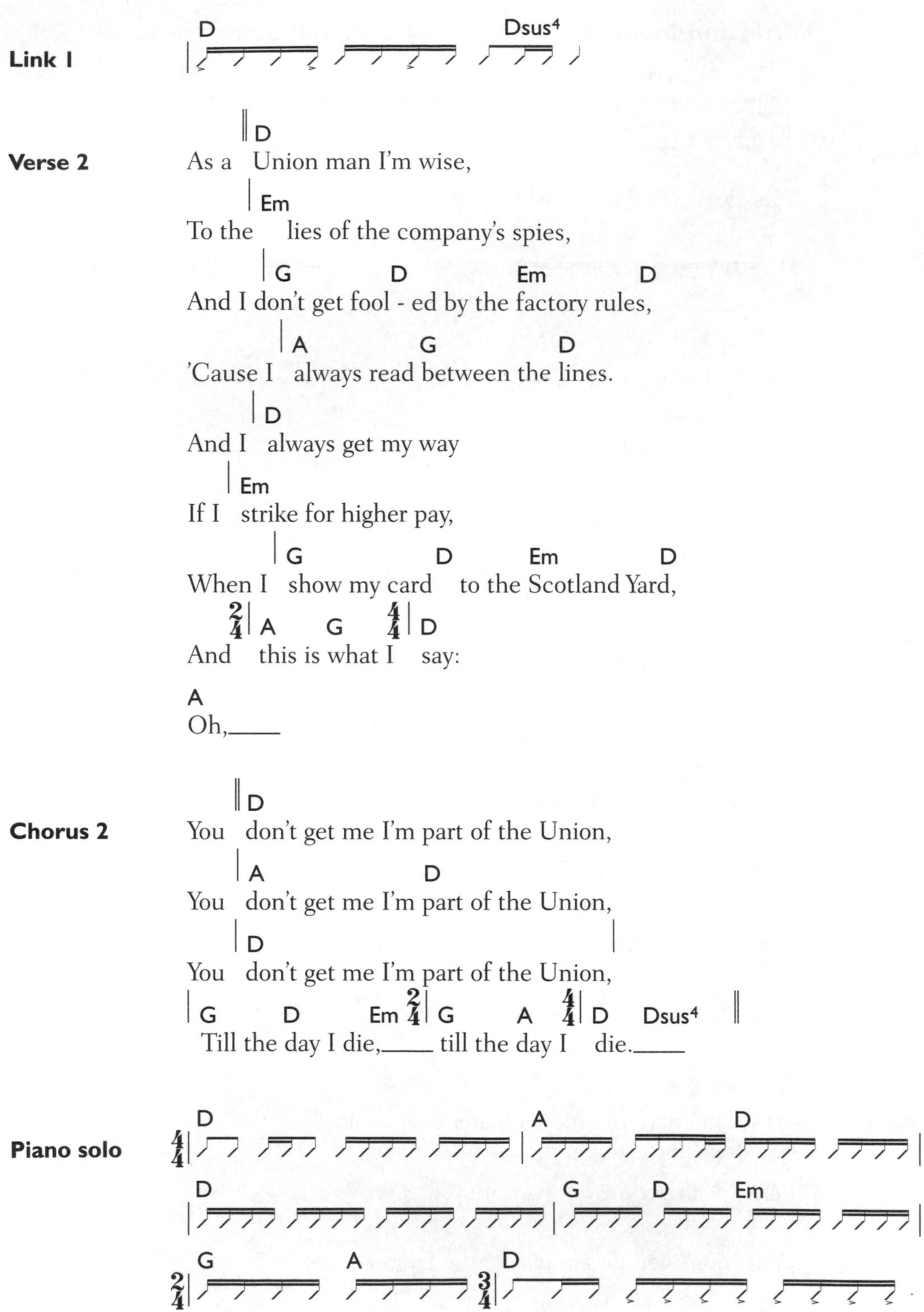
Link 1
D Dsus4
Verse 2
D
As a Union man I'm wise,
Em
To the lies of the company's spies,
G D Em D
And I don't get fool - ed by the factory rules,
A G D
'Cause I always read between the lines.
D
And I always get my way
Em
If I strike for higher pay,
G D Em D
When I show my card to the Scotland Yard,
2/4 A G 4/4 D
And this is what I say:
A
Oh,
Chorus 2
D
You don't get me I'm part of the Union,
A D
You don't get me I'm part of the Union,
D
You don't get me I'm part of the Union,
G D Em 2/4 G A 4/4 D Dsus4
Till the day I die, till the day I die.
Piano solo
4/4 D A D
D G D Em
2/4 G A 3/4 D

Verse 3

```
                 ‖D
Before the   Union did appear,
         |Em
My life     was half as clear,
             |G          D             Em           D
Now I've   got the po - wer to the working hour,
      |A          G          D
And   every other day of the year.
   |D
So   though I'm a working man,
       |Em
I can   ruin the government's plan,
     |G      D              Em           D
I'm   not too hard, but the side of my car
            3/4|A          G        D
Makes me     some kind of   super - man.
6/4|A7
  Oh,________
```

Chorus 3

```
     ‖D
You   don't get me I'm part of the Union,
     |A                 D
You   don't get me I'm part of the Union,
     |D
You   don't get me I'm part of the Union,
|G     D      Em   |G     A     D
 Till the day I die,    till the day I die.
     |D
You   don't get me I'm part of the Union,
     |A                 D
You   don't get me I'm part of the Union,
     |D                               |
You   don't get me I'm part of the Union,
|G     D      Em   |G     A    D   A7   D ‖
 Till the day I die,    till the day I die.____
```

THE QUEEN AND THE SOLDIER

Words and Music by Suzanne Vega

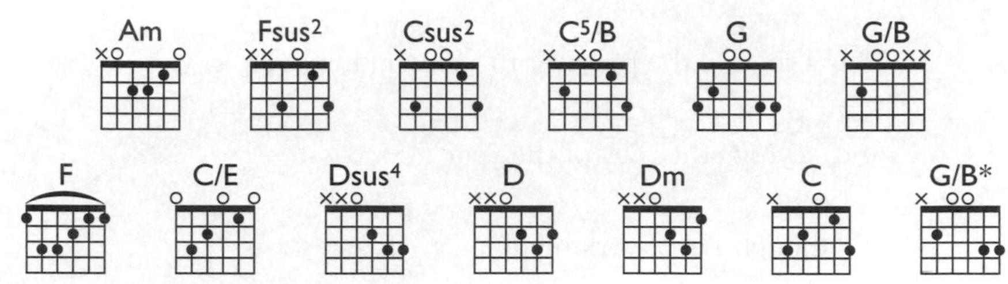

Capo 2nd Fret

♩ = 148

Intro

3/4 ‖: Am | Am | Fsus^2 | Fsus^2 |
fingerpicking

| Csus^2 | C^5/B | Csus^2 | [1.] G :‖ [2.] Csus^2 |

Verse 1

‖ Am | Am | Fsus^2 | Fsus^2
The soldier came knocking up - on the Queen's door,
| Csus^2 | C^5/B | Csus^2 | G
He said "I am not fighting for you any more."
| Am | Am | Fsus^2 | Fsus^2
And the Queen knew she'd seen his face someplace be - fore,
| Csus^2 | G/B | Csus^2 | Csus^2
And slowly she let him in - side.___

Verse 2

‖ Am | Am | Fsus^2 | Fsus^2
He said, "I've watched your palace up here on the hill,
| Csus^2 | G/B | Csus^2 | G
And I've wondered who's the woman for whom we all kill?
| Am | Am | Fsus^2 | Fsus^2
But I am leaving to - morrow, and you can do what you will,
| Csus^2 | G/B | Csus^2 | Csus^2 ‖
Only first, I am asking you, why?"___

Chorus 1

| F | F | C/E | C/E |
And down the long narrow hall he was led
| Dsus^{4} | Dsus^{4} | D | Dm
Into her room with her tapestries red,
| Am | Am | Fsus^{2} | Fsus^{2} |
And she never once took the crown from her head,
| Csus^{2} | G/B | Csus^{2} | Csus^{2} | Csus^{2} | Csus^{2}
She asked him there to sit down.

Verse 3

‖ Am | Am | Fsus^{2} | Fsus^{2}
He said, "I see you now, and you are so very young,
| Csus^{2} | C^{5}/B | Csus^{2} | G
But I've seen more battles lost, that I have battles won,
| Am | Am | Fsus^{2} | Fsus^{2}
And I've got this intui - tion, says it's all for your fun,
| Csus^{2} | G/B | Csus^{2} | Csus^{2}
And now will you___ tell me why?"

Verse 4

‖ Am | Am | Fsus^{2} | Fsus^{2}
Well the young queen she fixed him with an arrogant eye,
| Csus^{2} | G/B | Csus^{2} | G
She said "You won't under - stand, and you may as well not try",
| Am | Am | Fsus^{2} | Fsus^{2}
But her face was a child's, and he thought she would cry,
| Csus^{2} | G/B | Csus^{2} | Csus^{2}
But she closed herself up like a fan.

Chorus 2

‖ F | F | C/E | C/E
And she said, "I have swallowed a secret burning thread,
| Dsus^{4} | Dsus^{4} | D | Dm
It cuts me in - side, and often I've bled",
| Am | Am | Fsus^{2} | Fsus^{2}
And he laid his hand then on the top of her head,
| Csus^{2} | C^{5}/B | Csus^{2} | Csus^{2} ‖
And he bowed her down to the ground.

Instrumental

```
F          F              C/E            C/E              Dsus4        Dsus4
Oooh.___________________________________________________
D          Dm             Am             Am               Fsus2
__________________________________________________________
Fsus2      Csus2          G/B            Csus2            Csus2
```

Verse 5

```
              ‖Am            |Am              |Fsus2           |Fsus2
"And tell me   how hungry     are you? How     weak you must    feel,
        |Csus2           |C5/B             |Csus2               |G
As you   are living here  alone and you are never revealed,__
       |Am                |Am   |Fsus2        |Fsus2
But I   won't march again   on    your battle - field."
        |Csus2            |G/B           |Csus2  |Csus2
And he   took her to the   window to see.____
```

Verse 6

```
           ‖Am           |Am                  |Fsus2        |Fsus2
And the     sun it was    gold, though the     sky it was    grey,
     |Csus2          |C/B               |Csus2          |G
And   she wanted      more than she      ever could      say,
           |Am             |Am                  |Fsus2               |Fsus2
But she     knew how it     frightened her and   she turned a - way,
     |Csus2              |G/B              |Csus2     |Csus2
And   would not look at   his face a - gain.
```

Chorus 3

```
                 ‖F              |F           |C/E          |C/E
And he said,     "I want to       live as      an honest     man,
    |Dsus4          |Dsus4            |D          |Dm
To   get all I de -  serve and to      give all I  can,
        |Am            |Am                |Fsus2               |Fsus2
And to   love a young   woman who I        don't understand,
     |Csus2            |G/B       |Csus2             |Csus2   |Csus2   |Csus2
Your  Highness, your    ways are   very strange."
```

Verse 7

```
          ‖ Am          | Am            | Fsus²                  | Fsus²
But the     crown, it had   fallen, and she   thought she would   break,
          | Csus²       | C⁵/B          | Csus²        | G
And she     stood there,   ashamed of the way   her heart   ached,
          | Am               | Am                 | Fsus²               | Fsus²
And she     took him to the    doorstep, and she   asked him to wait,____
            | Csus²      | C⁵/B        | Csus²    | Csus²
She would     only be a    moment in - side.__
```

Verse 8

```
      ‖ Am        | Am              | F          | F
And     out in the   distance her   order was   heard
          | C            | G/B*        | C                | G
And the     soldier was   killed still   waiting for her   word,
                 | Am             | Am                 | F                    | F
And while the      Queen went on    strangling in the   solitude she pre - ferred,
    | C       | G/B*           | C        | G    ‖
The   battle          continued   on.____________
```

Outro

```
F         F           C/E         C/E         Dsus⁴       Dsus⁴
|♪ ♫ ♫ |♫ ♫ ♫ |♫ ♫ ♫ |♫ ♫ ♫ |♫ ♫ ♫ |♫ ♫ ♫ |
Oooh...________________________________________________

D         Dm          Am          Am          Fsus²       Fsus²
|♫ ♫ ♫ |♫ ♫ ♫ |♫ ♫ ♫ |♫ ♫ ♫ |♫ ♫ ♫ |♫ ♫ ♫ |

Csus²     G/B         C           Csus²       C           Csus²
|♫ ♫ ♫ |♫ ♫ ♫ |♫ ♫ ♫ |♪ ♫ ♪ ‖: ♫ ♫ ♫ |♪ ♫ ♪ :‖
```

Repeat to fade

RISING FOR THE MOON

Words and Music by Sandy Denny

Cadd9 Em7 Am11 G* D G/B
A7sus4 G D7sus4 C Em Am Am7
2fr
Capo 2nd Fret
♩ = 125
Intro
Cadd9 Em7 Am11 G*
D Cadd9 G/B A7sus4
Verse 1
G D7sus4 G G G/B C
I travel ov - er the sea and ride the rolling sky,
G D7sus4 G G/B C D
For that's the way it is, that is my__ for - tune.
G D7sus4 G G/B C Em C
There are many ears to please, many peo - ple's love to try
G D G G
And every day's begun rising for the moon.
Verse 2
G D7sus4 G G G/B C
There's a heart in eve - ry__ place, there's a tear for each fare - well,
G D7sus4 G G/B C D
For that's the way it is, that is my__ for - tune.
G D7sus4 G G/B C Em C
I'll lure you as the lace that the way - ward gypsies sell,
G D G G
With the sinking of the sun, rising of__ the moon.__

Chorus 1

```
| C              | C                 | G              | G
  Rising for the   moon, the sun has   set and it is   dark,
          | C    Em        | Am                | G             | D        | D
But the    star of the en - chanted tune is    bright as any    spark.____
    | G                | G      G/B   | C        Em       | C
The   chorus of the    dusk re   -    gail the evening    lark
      | G                   | D                  | G          | G          ||
Whose   every day does start    rising for the    moon.____
```

Instrumental

```
4/4 | C           |    | C           |    ||
|: G  | G  | C  Em  | Am7 |
| G  | D  | D  :| G  | G
```

Verse 3

```
  || G            D7sus4  | G        | G        G/B     | C
We    travel ov - er the     sea and   ride the rolling    sky
    | G               D7sus4    | G         G/B     | C      | D
For   that's the way it            is,   that is our__ for - tune.
              | G             D7sus4  | G       G/B           | C    Em  | C
There are   many ears to          please, many peo - ple's love    to try
    | G                | D             | G             | G        ||
And   every day's begun    rising for      the moon.
```

Chorus 2

```
| C              | C                 | G              | G
  Rising for the   moon, the sun has   set and it is   dark,
          | C    Em        | Am                | G             | D        | D
But the    star of the en - chanted tune is    bright as any    spark.____
    | G                | G      G/B   | C        Em       | C
The   chorus of the    dusk re   -    gail the evening    lark,
      | G                   | D                  | G          | G          |
Whose   every day does start    rising for the    moon.____
| C              | C                 | G              | G
  Rising for the   moon, the sun has   set and it is   dark,
          | C    Em        | Am                | G             | D        | D
But the    star of the en - chanted tune is    bright as any    spark.____
    | G                | G      G/B   | C       Em       | C        | C
The   chorus of the    dusk re   -    gail the evening    lark,_______
      | G                   | D                  | G          | G     | G     | G(fermata)   ||
Whose   every day does start    rising for the    moon.____
```

ROSEMARY LANE

Traditional. Arranged by James Yorkston

G5 G5* F G G7 G* Dm/F (5fr)

Tune guitar

① = D ④ = D

② = B ⑤ = G

③ = G ⑥ = D (lowest string)

Capo 2nd Fret

♩= 88

Intro

G5
2/4 | / / / / / / / / | / / / / / / / / |
fingerpicking

Verse 1

```
      ||G5      |G5*       |F          |G      |G
When  I__ was in  service in  Rosemary Lane
  |G5*  G7  G*  |G*     |F          |G     |G
I kept the good will  of my mas - ter Amber - dine
    |G5* G7    G*       |F               |Dm/F  |Dm/F
Un - til a young sailor, he  came there to stay
    |G          |G          |F          |G    |G    |G    |G
And  that was the be - ginning of  my misery.____
```

Verse 2

```
     ||G5       |G5*       |F          |G     |G
He  called for a  candle to  light him to  bed,
     |G5*         G7      |G*            |F        |G      |G
And  likewise a silk hand - kerchief to  tie up his  hair,
   |G5*  G7  |G*     |F             |Dm/F  |Dm/F
To  tie up his  hair as  sailors will  do
     |G            |G5*           |F           |G     |G    |G    |G
Says  he,"Pretty Pol - ly, won't you  come to bed  too?"
```

Verse 3

```
     ||G5                      |G5*      |F              |G        |G
This  girl being young and  foolish,  she thought it no harm
     |G5*     G7   |G*   |F            |G      |G
To jump in - to bed to keep herself warm,
     |G5*    G7     |G*        |F          |Dm/F   |Dm/F
But what was done next I will  never  de - clare,
     |G                |G5*           |F             |G
But I wish that short night had been  seven long  year.
```

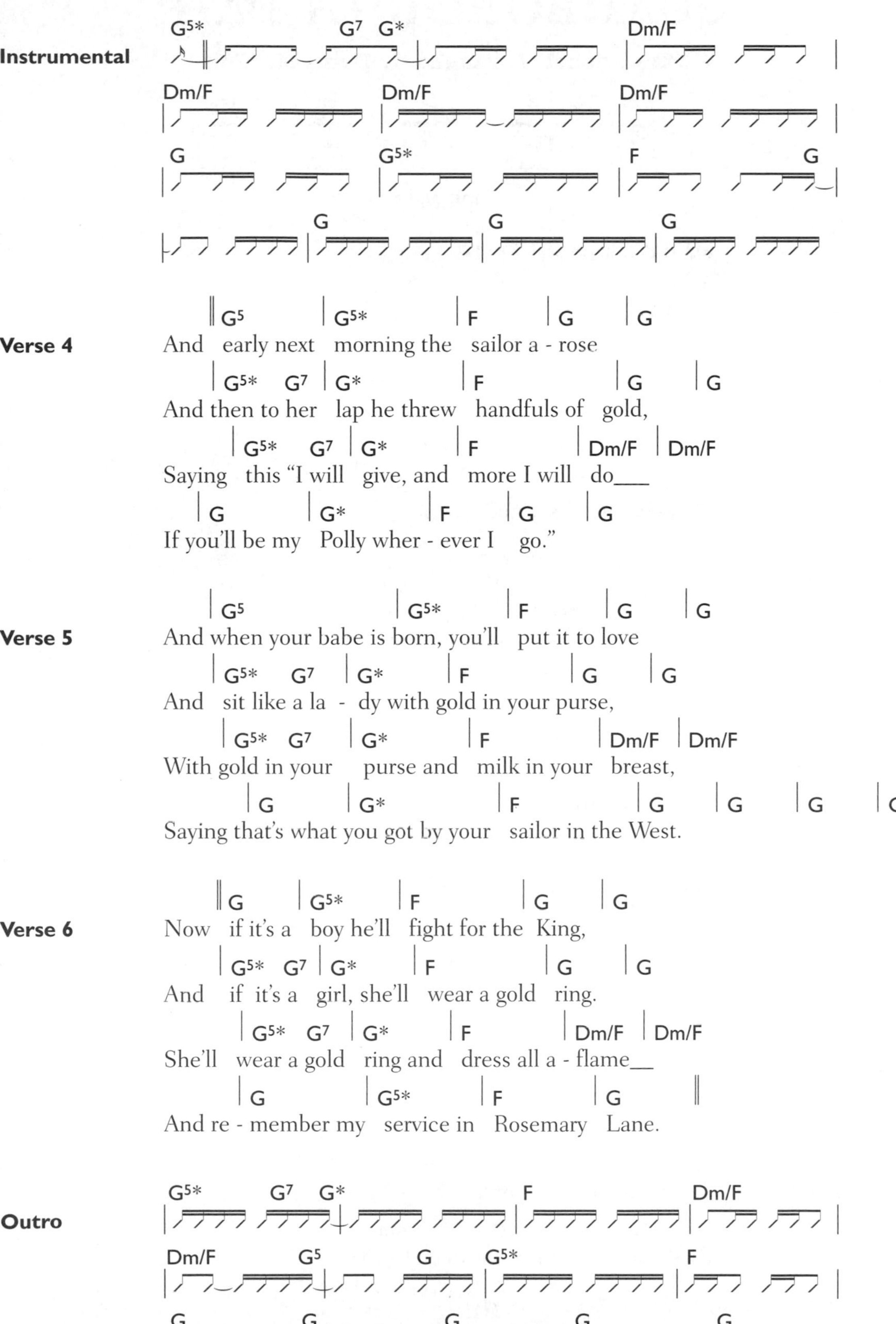
Instrumental
G5* G7 G* Dm/F
Dm/F Dm/F Dm/F
G G5* F G
G G G
Verse 4
G5 G5* F G G
And early next morning the sailor a - rose
G5* G7 G* F G G
And then to her lap he threw handfuls of gold,
G5* G7 G* F Dm/F Dm/F
Saying this "I will give, and more I will do___
G G* F G G
If you'll be my Polly wher - ever I go."
Verse 5
G5 G5* F G G
And when your babe is born, you'll put it to love
G5* G7 G* F G G
And sit like a la - dy with gold in your purse,
G5* G7 G* F Dm/F Dm/F
With gold in your purse and milk in your breast,
G G* F G G G G
Saying that's what you got by your sailor in the West.
Verse 6
G G5* F G G
Now if it's a boy he'll fight for the King,
G5* G7 G* F G G
And if it's a girl, she'll wear a gold ring.
G5* G7 G* F Dm/F Dm/F
She'll wear a gold ring and dress all a - flame__
G G5* F G
And re - member my service in Rosemary Lane.
Outro
G5* G7 G* F Dm/F
Dm/F G5 G G5* F
G G G G G

SCARBOROUGH FAIR

Traditional. Arranged by Ewan MacColl

Am G D Em Dm

Capo 3rd Fret

6/8 feel but no strict pulse

Verse 1

```
Am            Am      G             Am
       Are you going to Scarborough Fair?
Am                    D         Am
Parsley, sage, rose - mary and thyme,
     Am               Em           G
Re - member me to one that lives there,
Am            D      Em           Am
For once she was a true love of mine.
```

Verse 2

```
Am                         D         Am
Tell her to make me a cambric shirt,
       Am                  D          Am
Pars - ley, sage, rose - mary and thyme,
        Am                        G
With - out any seam or needle - work
Am               D    Em          Am
And then she'll be a true love of mine.
```

Verse 3

```
Am                       D          Am
Tell her to wash it in yonder dry well,
Am                    D         Am
Parsley, sage, rose - mary and thyme,
        Am                         Em          G
Where water ne'er sprung, nor drop of rain fell
     Am          D    Em          Am
And then she'll be a true love of mine.
```

Verse 4

```
Am                    G       Am
Tell her to dry it on yonder thorn,
       Am                  D          Am
Pars - ley, sage, rose - mary and thyme
```

cont.

          Am   G
Which never bore blossom since Adam was born

      Am   D   Em   Am
And then she'll be a true love of mine.

Verse 5

    Am   G   Am
Oh   will you find me an acre of land?

        Am   D   Am
Pars - ley, sage, rose - mary and thyme,

      Am   G
Be - tween the sea foam and the sea sand

    Am   D   Em   Am
Or never be a true   lover of mine.

Verse 6

Am   G   Am
Oh will you plough it with a lamb's horn?

Am   D   Am
Parsley, sage, rose - mary and thyme,

      Am   G
And sow it all over with one pepper - corn

    Am   Dm Em   Am
Or never be   a true lover of mine.

Verse 7

Am   G   Am
Oh will you reap it with a sickle of leather?

Am   D   Am
Parsley, sage, rose - mary and thyme,

      Am   G
And tie it all up with a peacock's feather

Am   D   Em   Am
Or never be a true lover of mine.

Verse 8

      Am   G   Am
And when you have done and   finished your work

Am   D   Am
Parsley, sage, rose - mary and thyme,

Am   G
Then come to me for your cambric shirt

Am   D   Em   Am
And you shall be a true love of mine.

SHE MOVED THROUGH THE FAIR

Traditional
Arranged by Padraic Colum

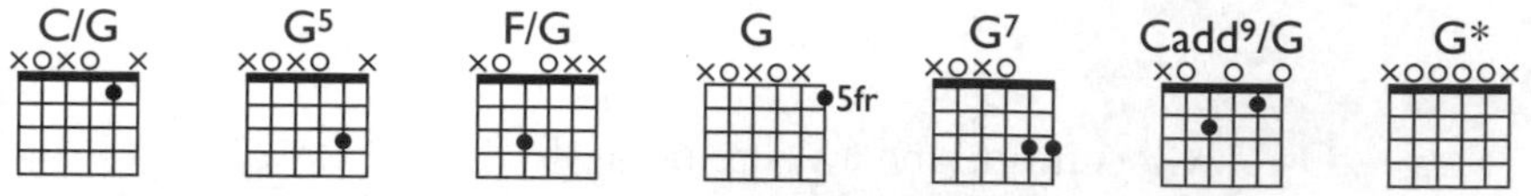

C/G G5 F/G G G7 Cadd9/G G*

Tune guitar
① = D ④ = D
② = B ⑤ = G
③ = G ⑥ = D (lowest string)

Capo 4th Fret

Intro 3/4 | G | C/G | G5 | F/G | G5 | G | G7 |
| Cadd9/G | G5 | G | G7 | Cadd9/G | G5 |
| C/G | G5 | F/G | G5 | G* F/G | G5 |

Verse 1

C/G G5 F/G G5
My young love said to me "My mother won't mind

G G7 Cadd9/G G5
And my father won't slight you for your lack of kind"

G G7 Cadd9/G G5
And she laid her hand on me, and this she did say

C/G G5 F/G G5 G* F/G G5
"It will not be long love, till our wedding day."

Verse 2

C/G G5 F/G G5
She stepped away from me and she went through the fair

G G7 Cadd9/G G5
And fondly I watched her move here and move there,

G G7 Cadd9/G G5
And then she went homeward with one star a - wake

C/G G5 F/G G5 G* F/G G5
As the swan in the evening moved over the lake.

Instrumental

G C/G G5 F/G G5 G G7

Cadd9/G G5 G G7 Cadd9/G G5

C/G G5 F/G G5 G* F/G G5

Verse 3

C/G G5 F/G G5
Last night she came to me, my true love came in

G G7 Cadd9/G G5
And so softly she came that her feet made no din____

G G7 Cadd9/G G5
And she laid her hand on me, and this she did say____

C/G G5 F/G G5 G* F/G G5
"It will not be long love, till our wedding day."

Outro

G* F/G G5 G* F/G G

rit.

SONG TO THE SIREN

Words and Music by Tim Buckley and Larry Beckett

Asus2 A/E E D/F♯ F♯m
A D5 Gsus2 Gadd9 D6/F♯

Tune guitar
① = E ④ = D
② = B ⑤ = A
③ = G ⑥ = D (lowest string)

Freely ♩ = c. 150 Capo 1st Fret

Intro
‖ Asus2 ‖
finger picking ad lib.

Verse 1
| A/E | E |
Long afloat on shipless oceans,
| D/F♯ | F♯m |
I did all my best to smile
| A | E |
'Til your singing eyes and fingers
| D5 | F♯m ‖
Drew me loving to your isle.

Chorus 1
| A | Gsus2 Gadd9 Gsus2 Gadd9 |
And you sang, "Sail to me,
| D6/F♯ | A |
Sail to me, let me en - fold you.
| F♯m | F♯m | E | D5 ‖
Here I am, here I am waiting to hold you."____

Verse 2
| Asus2 | E |
Did I dream you dreamed about me?
| D5 | F♯m |
Were you hare when I was fox?
| Asus2 | E |
Now my foolish boat is leaning
| D5 | F♯m ‖
Broken, lovelorn on your rocks.

Chorus 2

| Asus2 | Gsus2 |
For you sing, "Touch me not,
| D/F# | A |
Touch me not, come back to - morrow;
| F#m | F#m | E | D5 | F#m
Oh my heart, oh my heart shies from the sorrow."________

Verse 3

‖ Asus2 | E | D5
But I'm as puzzled as the new born child
| F#m |
I'm as riddled as the tide:
| A | E |
Should I stand amid the breakers,
| D5 | F#m ‖
Or should I lie with death my bride?

Chorus 3

| Asus2 | Gadd9 |
Hear me sing, "Swim to me,
| D/F# | A |
Swim to me, let me en - fold you:
| F#m | F#m | E | D5 | F#m ‖
Here I am, here I am, waiting to hold________ you.__

THE STREETS OF LONDON

Words and Music by Ralph McTell

C G G6 Am Em F

C/G G7 G13 C/B Am/G D7/F♯ Csus4

♩ = 79 **Capo 3rd Fret**

Intro

4/4 | C G G6 | Am Em |

fingerpicked

| F C/G | G G7 C ||

Verse 1

| C G | Am Em |
Have you seen the old man in the closed down market

| F C/G | F G13
Kicking up the pa - per with his worn out shoes?

| C G |
In his eyes you see no pride

| Am Em |
And held loosely at his side

| F C/G | G7 C 2/4 | C
Yesterday's paper, telling yesterday's news.

Chorus 1

4/4 | F Em | C C/B Am Am/G |
So how can you tell me you're lone - ly?____

| D7/F♯ | G G6 |
And say for you that the sun don't shine?____

| C G G6 | Am Em |
Let me take you by the hand and lead you through the streets of London,

| F C/G | G7 C ||
Show you some - thing to make you change your mind.

Link 1

| C G G6 | Am G ||

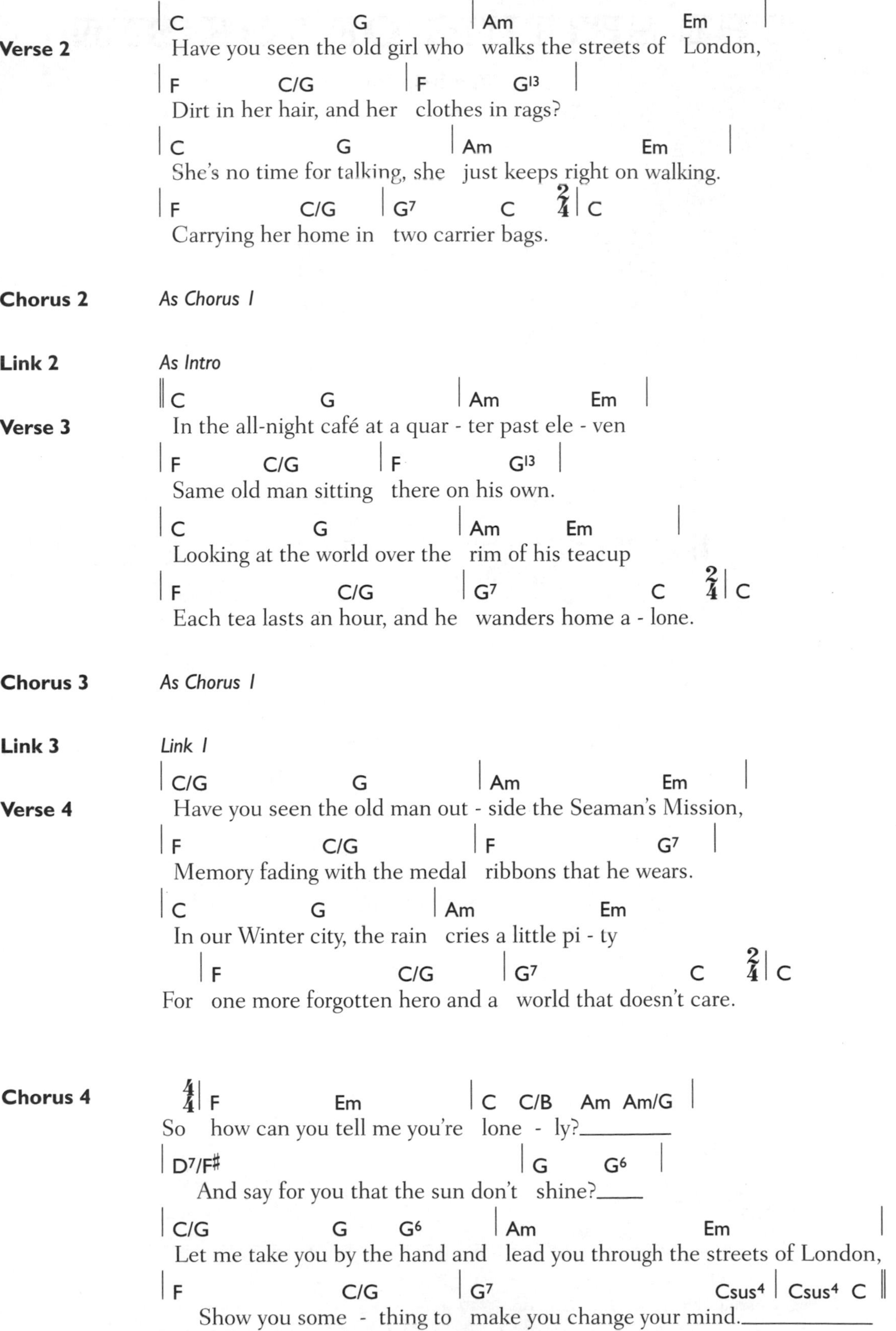

Verse 2
C G Am Em
Have you seen the old girl who walks the streets of London,
F C/G F G13
Dirt in her hair, and her clothes in rags?
C G Am Em
She's no time for talking, she just keeps right on walking.
F C/G G7 C 2/4 C
Carrying her home in two carrier bags.
Chorus 2
As Chorus 1
Link 2
As Intro
Verse 3
C G Am Em
In the all-night café at a quar - ter past ele - ven
F C/G F G13
Same old man sitting there on his own.
C G Am Em
Looking at the world over the rim of his teacup
F C/G G7 C 2/4 C
Each tea lasts an hour, and he wanders home a - lone.
Chorus 3
As Chorus 1
Link 3
Link 1
Verse 4
C/G G Am Em
Have you seen the old man out - side the Seaman's Mission,
F C/G F G7
Memory fading with the medal ribbons that he wears.
C G Am Em
In our Winter city, the rain cries a little pi - ty
F C/G G7 C 2/4 C
For one more forgotten hero and a world that doesn't care.
Chorus 4
4/4 F Em C C/B Am Am/G
So how can you tell me you're lone - ly?
D7/F# G G6
And say for you that the sun don't shine?
C/G G G6 Am Em
Let me take you by the hand and lead you through the streets of London,
F C/G G7 Csus4 Csus4 C
Show you some - thing to make you change your mind.

THE SETTING OF THE SUN

Traditional
Arranged by Seth Lakeman

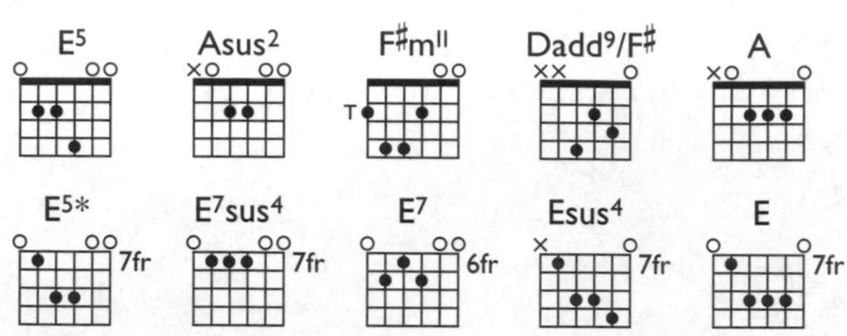

Capo 1st Fret

♩ = 84

Intro 4/4 ‖: E5 / / / / / / / / / / / / Asus2 / / / | E5 / / / / / / / / / / / / Asus2 / / / :‖

Verse 1

‖ E5 Asus2 | E5
Come all__ young fellows that carry a gun,

Asus2 | E5 Asus2 | E5
Beware of late shooting when the daylight is done.

Asus2 3/4 | Asus2 4/4 | F#m11 Asus2 | E5 Asus2 |
It is my own reckoning that many hazards they may run.

Asus2 3/4 | Asus2 4/4 | Dadd9 A | E5 Asus2 | E5
I shot my true love at the setting of the sun.

Verse 2

Asus2 ‖ E5 Asus2 | E5
In a sho - wer of rain my dar - ling did lie,

Asus2 | E5 Asus2 | E5
All un - der the bushes to keep herself dry.

Asus2 3/4 | Asus2 4/4 | F#m11 Asus2 | E5 Asus2 | E5
Her head in her apron I thought her as a swan.

Asus2 3/4 | Asus2 4/4 | Dadd9/F# A 3/4 ‖ E5* E7sus4 E7 E7sus4 E7 |
I shot my true love at the setting of the sun.

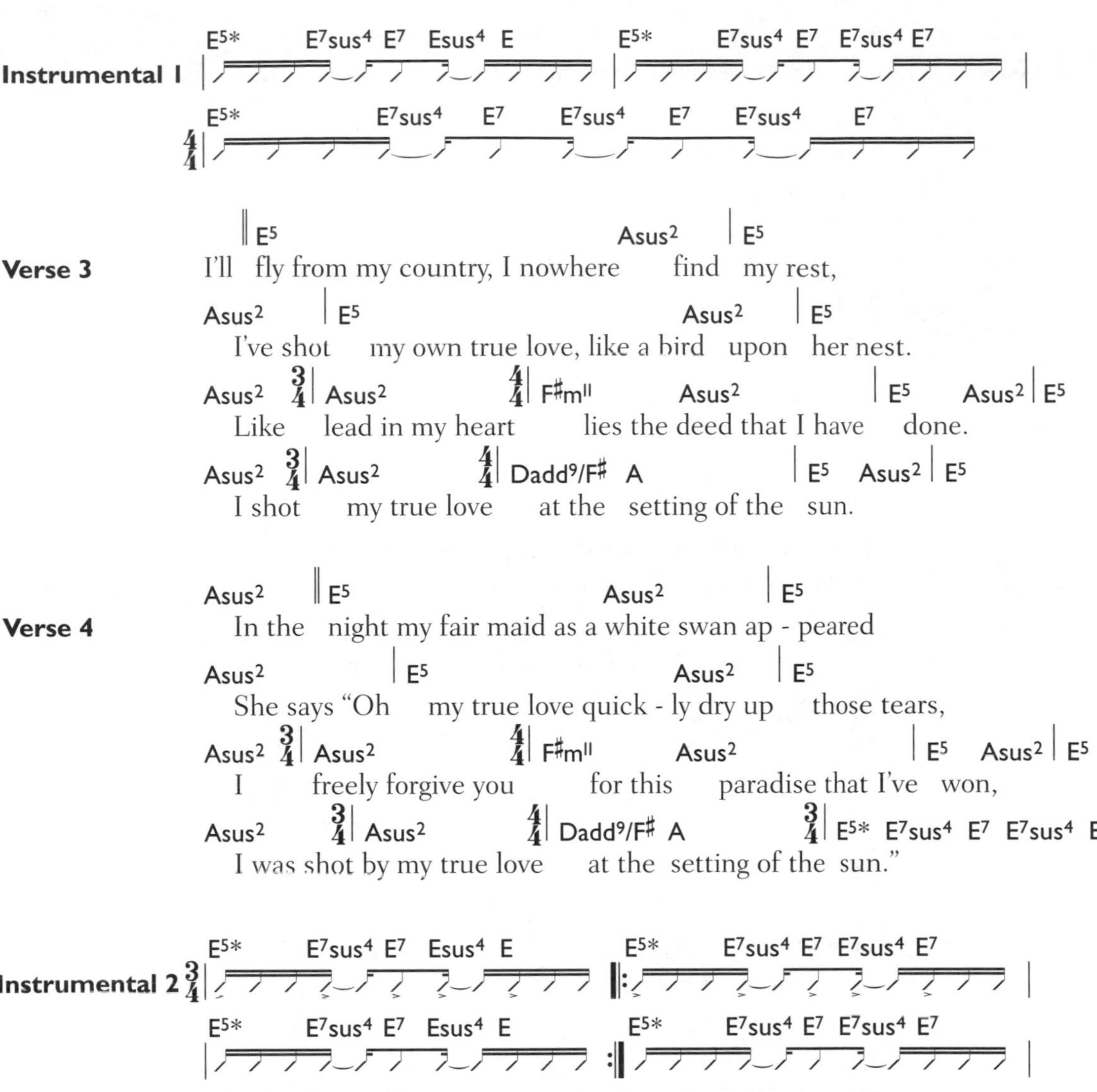
Instrumental 1
E5* E7sus4 E7 Esus4 E E5* E7sus4 E7 E7sus4 E7
E5* E7sus4 E7 E7sus4 E7 E7sus4 E7
Verse 3
E5 Asus2 E5
I'll fly from my country, I nowhere find my rest,
Asus2 E5 Asus2 E5
I've shot my own true love, like a bird upon her nest.
Asus2 Asus2 F#m11 Asus2 E5 Asus2 E5
Like lead in my heart lies the deed that I have done.
Asus2 Asus2 Dadd9/F# A E5 Asus2 E5
I shot my true love at the setting of the sun.
Verse 4
Asus2 E5 Asus2 E5
In the night my fair maid as a white swan ap - peared
Asus2 E5 Asus2 E5
She says "Oh my true love quick - ly dry up those tears,
Asus2 Asus2 F#m11 Asus2 E5 Asus2 E5
I freely forgive you for this paradise that I've won,
Asus2 Asus2 Dadd9/F# A E5* E7sus4 E7 E7sus4 E7
I was shot by my true love at the setting of the sun."
Instrumental 2
E5* E7sus4 E7 Esus4 E E5* E7sus4 E7 E7sus4 E7
E5* E7sus4 E7 Esus4 E E5* E7sus4 E7 E7sus4 E7
E5* E7sus4 E7 E7sus4 E7 E7sus4 E7

Verse 5

```
            || E5                                  Asus2      | E5
Oh the   years they pass and leave me      lonely   and sad.
Asus2  | E5                                  Asus2           | E5
   I can   never love again for none make me glad.
Asus2 3/4| Asus2              4/4| F#m11         Asus2              | E5   Asus2 | E5
   I'll wait     and expect you        until my work down here is done,
Asus2        3/4| Asus2         4/4| Dadd9/F#  A        3/4| E5*
   I'll meet          my true love        at the rising of the   sun.
```

Outro

```
        E7sus4 E7 E7sus4  E7   || E5* E7sus4  E7   Esus4   E   | E5*
The sun     is  set  -  ting,      go  -  ing  way    on   down
E7sus4  E7       E7sus4 E7  | E5*  E7sus4  E7   Esus4   E   | E5*
Ov    -   er the val  -  ley,        go   -   ing  way     on   down
E7sus4  E7    E7sus4  E7  | E5        E7sus4  E7   Esus4   E  |
   Bow   to her,____  gold - en maid - en,
| E5* E7sus4        E7  E7sus4  E7 | E5*     E7sus4  E7         Esus4    E     |
           Gold - en maid - en   wow, go   -   ing way on       down,
| E5* E7sus4        E7  E7sus4  E7 | E5*     E7sus4  E7        Esus4    E    |
           Gold - en maid - en   wow, ov   -   er the val   -   ley,
| E5* E7sus4        E7  E7sus4  E7 | E5*     E7sus4  E7         Esus4    E     |
           Gold - en maid - en   wow, go   -   ing way on       down,
| E5* E7sus4        E7  E7sus4  E7 | E5*     E7sus4  E7        Esus4    E    |
           Gold - en maid - en   wow, ov   -   er the val   -   ley,
| E5* E7sus4        E7sus4  E7     4/4| E5*     E7sus4  E7  E7sus4  E7  E7sus4  E7 | E5  |
           Bow to her,____    the     sun is set   -   ting.________________
```

THIS LAND IS YOUR LAND

Traditional
Arranged by Woody Guthrie

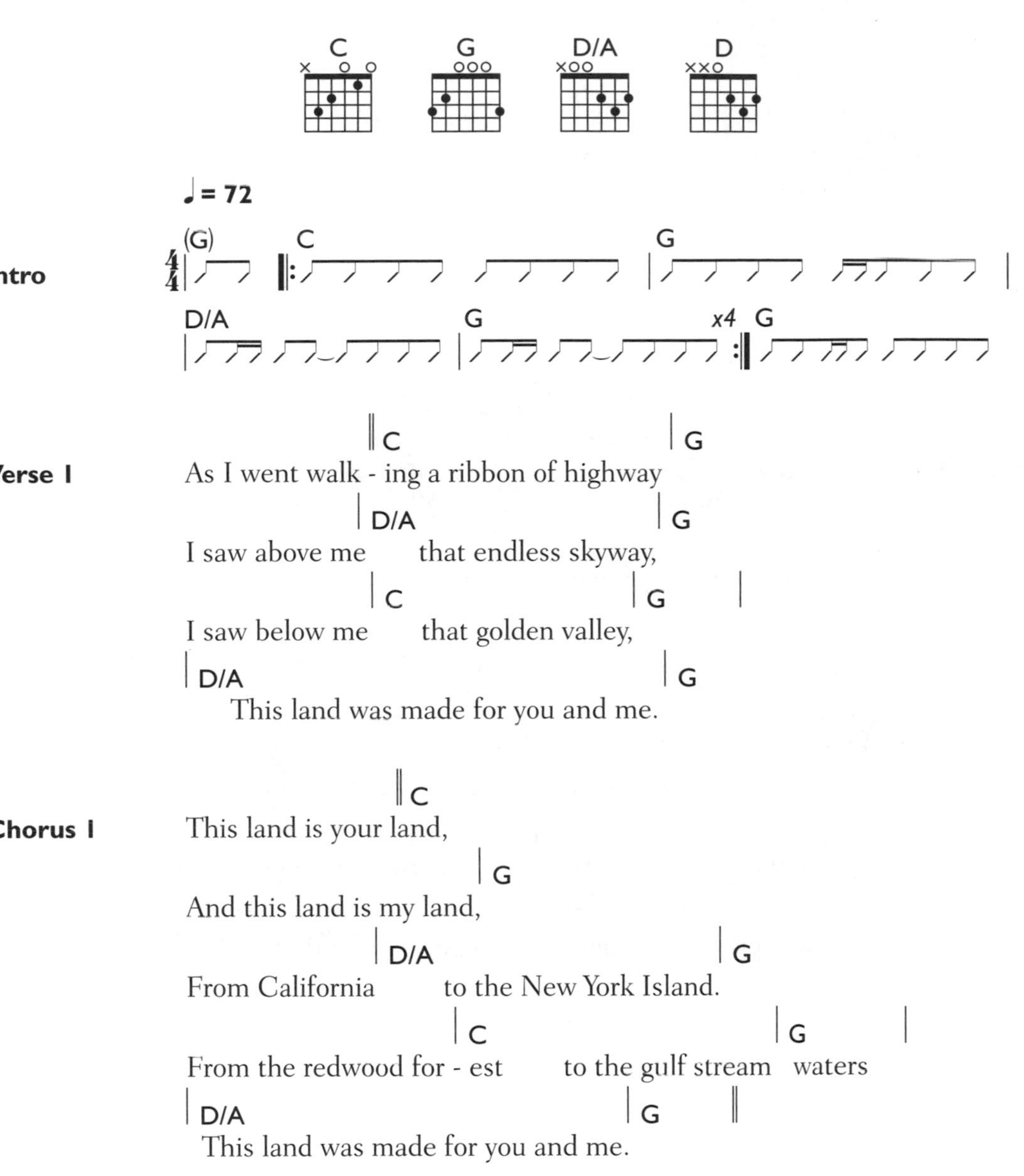
C
G
D/A
D
♩ = 72
Intro
(G)
C
G
D/A
G
x4
G
Verse 1
C G
As I went walk - ing a ribbon of highway
D/A G
I saw above me that endless skyway,
C G
I saw below me that golden valley,
D/A G
This land was made for you and me.
Chorus 1
C
This land is your land,
G
And this land is my land,
D/A G
From California to the New York Island.
C G
From the redwood for - est to the gulf stream waters
D/A G
This land was made for you and me.

Link 1

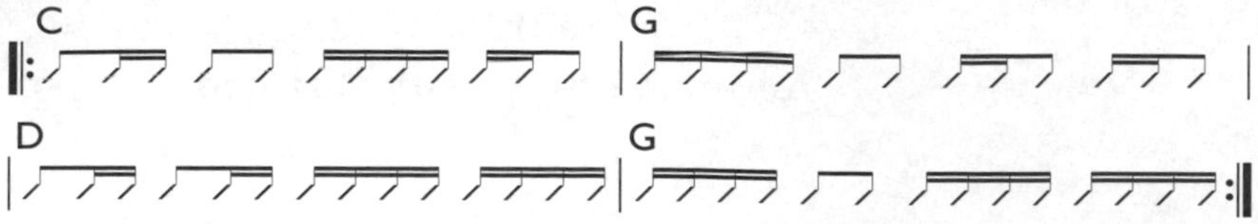

Verse 2

C G
I roamed and rambled and followed my foot - steps
D G
To the sunny bright sands of her diamond deserts,
C G
And all a - round me, a voice came singing,
D/A G
Singing 'This land was made for you and me.'

Chorus 2 *As Chorus 1*

Link 2

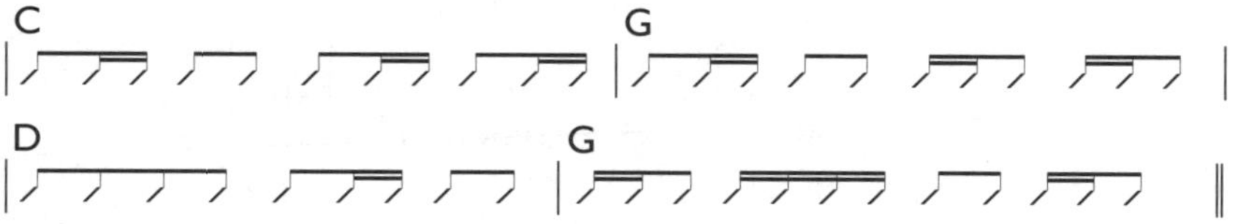

Verse 3

2/4 G 4/4 C G
It was early one morn - ing, I was a-stroll - ing,
D G
With the wheat fields wav - ing, and the dust clouds rolling,
C G D G
As the fog was lift - ing, a voice comes chanting…

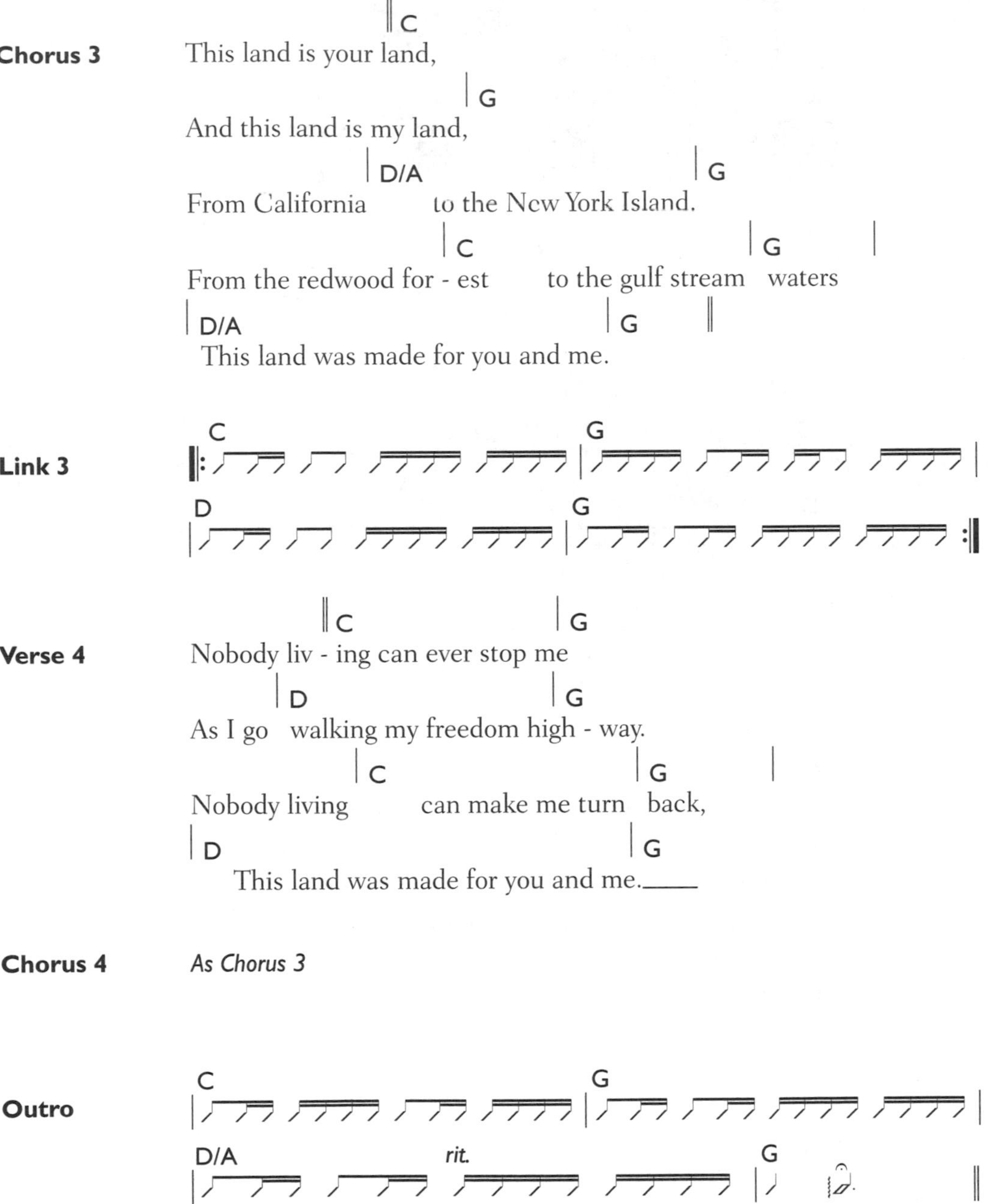
Chorus 3
C
This land is your land,
G
And this land is my land,
D/A
G
From California to the New York Island.
C
G
From the redwood for - est to the gulf stream waters
D/A
G
This land was made for you and me.
Link 3
C
G
D
G
Verse 4
C
G
Nobody liv - ing can ever stop me
D
G
As I go walking my freedom high - way.
C
G
Nobody living can make me turn back,
D
G
This land was made for you and me.
Chorus 4
As Chorus 3
Outro
C
G
D/A
rit.
G

UNIVERSE & U

Words and Music by Katie Tunstall, Hadrian Garrard and Frederik Ball

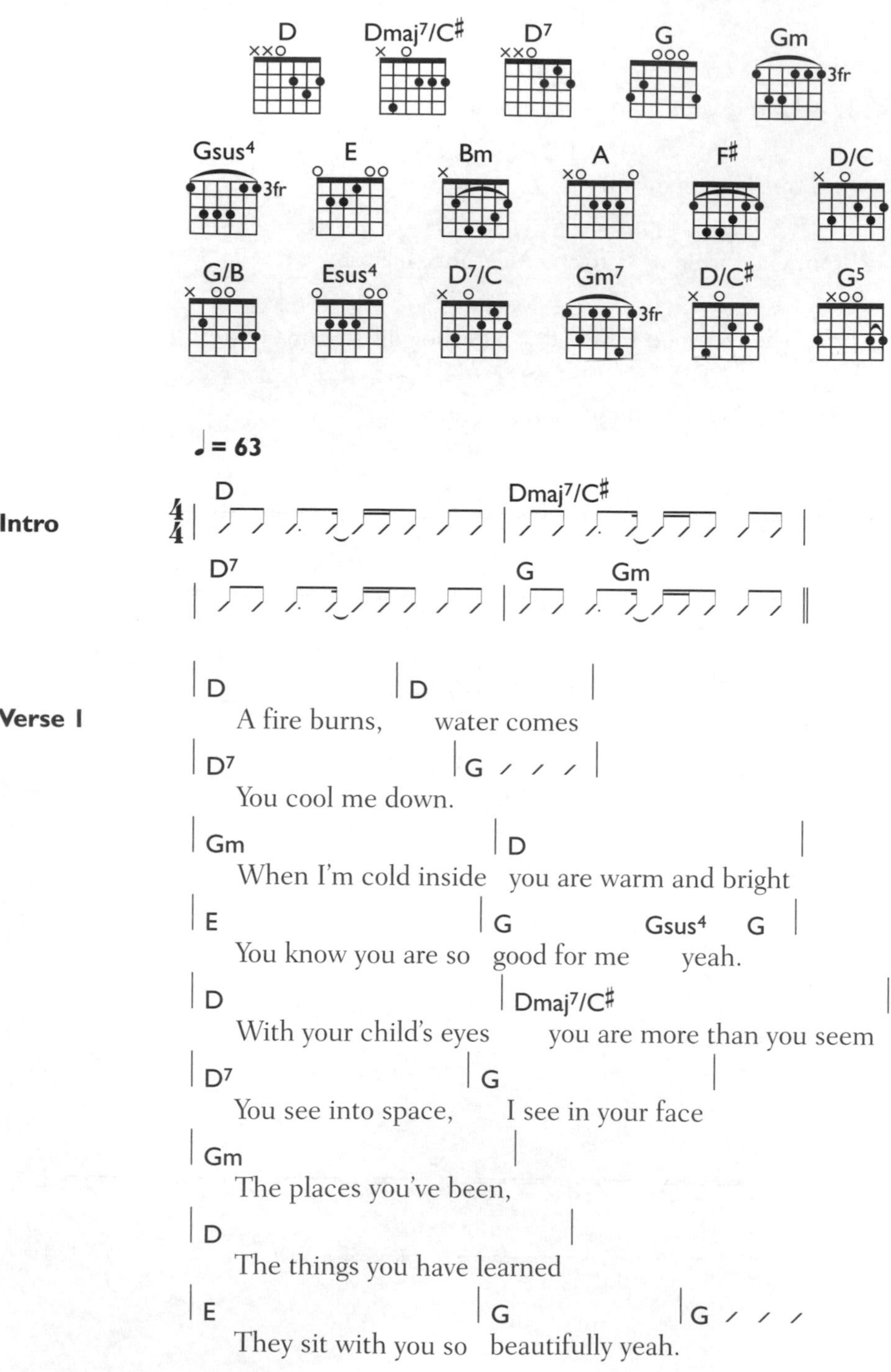
D
Dmaj7/C#
D7
G
Gm
3fr
Gsus4
3fr
E
Bm
A
F#
D/C
G/B
Esus4
D7/C
Gm7
3fr
D/C#
G5
♩= 63
Intro
D
Dmaj7/C#
D7
G
Gm
Verse 1
D
D
A fire burns, water comes
D7
G
You cool me down.
Gm
D
When I'm cold inside you are warm and bright
E
G
Gsus4
G
You know you are so good for me yeah.
D
Dmaj7/C#
With your child's eyes you are more than you seem
D7
G
You see into space, I see in your face
Gm
The places you've been,
D
The things you have learned
E
G
G
They sit with you so beautifully yeah.

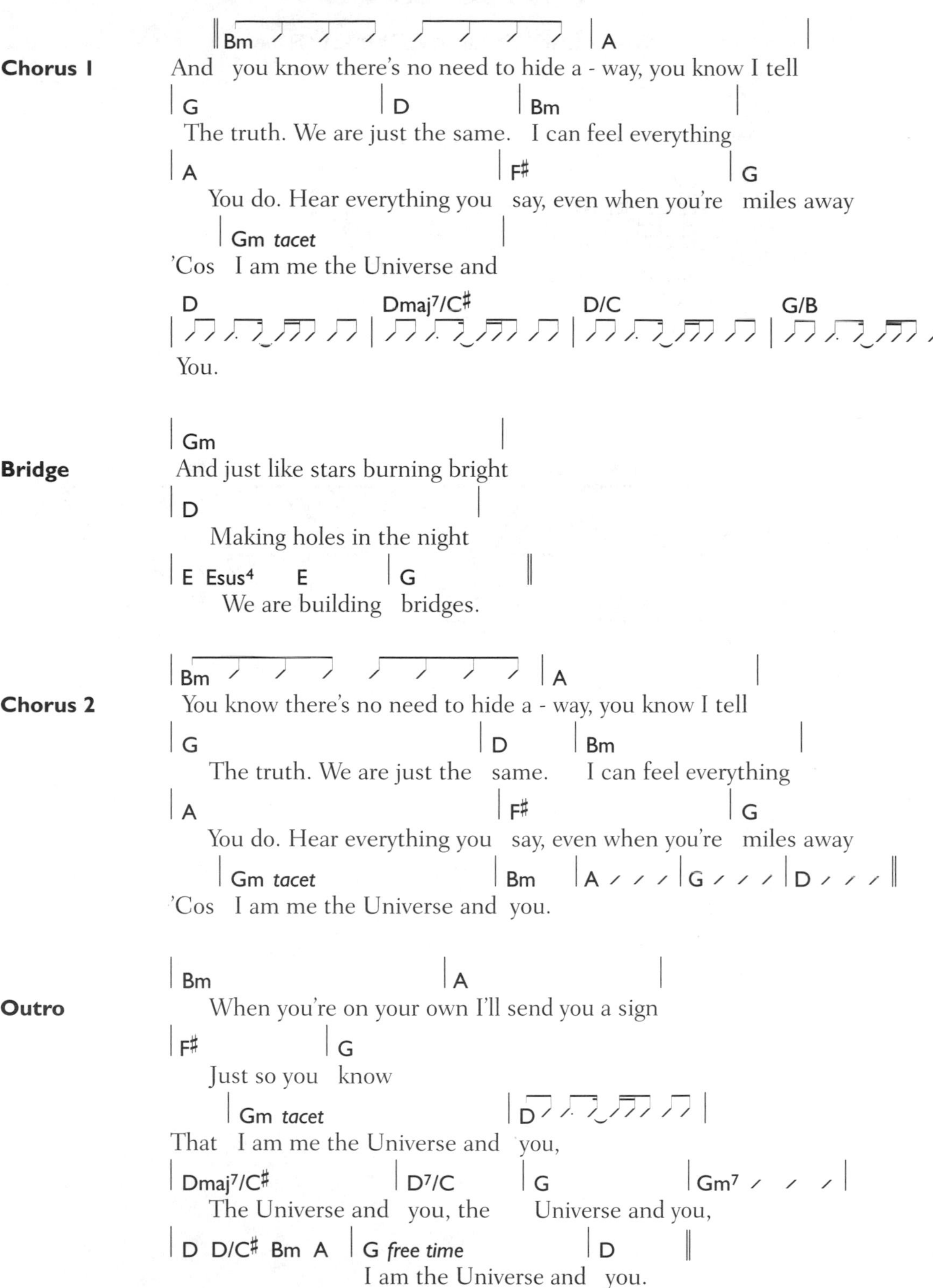
Chorus 1
Bm A
And you know there's no need to hide a - way, you know I tell
G D Bm
The truth. We are just the same. I can feel everything
A F# G
You do. Hear everything you say, even when you're miles away
Gm tacet
'Cos I am me the Universe and
D Dmaj7/C# D/C G/B
You.
Bridge
Gm
And just like stars burning bright
D
Making holes in the night
E Esus4 E G
We are building bridges.
Chorus 2
Bm A
You know there's no need to hide a - way, you know I tell
G D Bm
The truth. We are just the same. I can feel everything
A F# G
You do. Hear everything you say, even when you're miles away
Gm tacet Bm A G D
'Cos I am me the Universe and you.
Outro
Bm A
When you're on your own I'll send you a sign
F# G
Just so you know
Gm tacet D
That I am me the Universe and you,
Dmaj7/C# D7/C G Gm7
The Universe and you, the Universe and you,
D D/C# Bm A G free time D
I am the Universe and you.

VOLCANO

Words and Music by Damien Rice

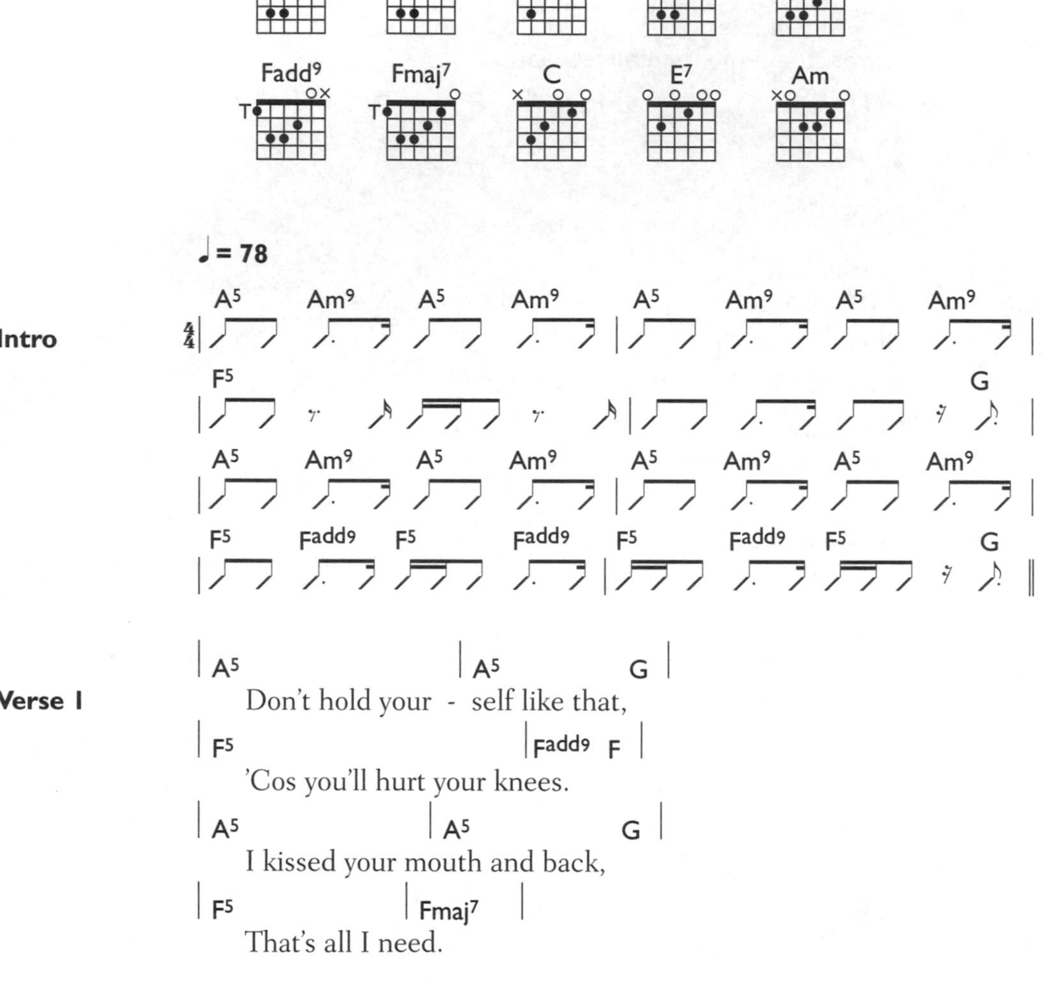

Verse 1

| A5 | A5 G |
Don't hold your - self like that,
| F5 | Fadd9 F |
'Cos you'll hurt your knees.
| A5 | A5 G |
I kissed your mouth and back,
| F5 | Fmaj7 |
That's all I need.

Pre-chorus 1

| G | Fadd9 |
Don't build your world around,
| G | Fadd9
Volcanoes melt you down.

Chorus 1

```
N.C.         G ‖ Am9
 And what I      am to you
          | Fmaj7
Is not real,
        G | Am9
What I      am to you,
          G   | Fmaj7
You do not need.
        G | Am9
What I      am to you,
        G        | Fmaj7
Is not what you     mean to me,
                 G   | Am9
But you give me miles and miles of mountains,
      | Fmaj7  N.C. ‖ Am9   | Am9   G |
And    I'll ask for the  sea.
```

Link

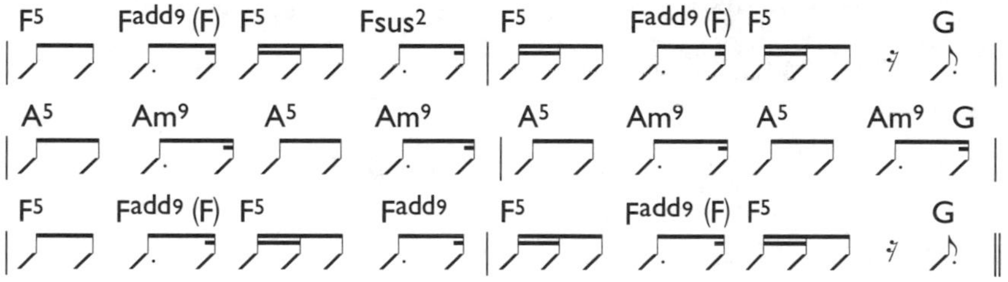

```
| F5  Fadd9 (F) F5  Fsus2 | F5  Fadd9 (F) F5  G |
| A5  Am9  A5  Am9 | A5  Am9  A5  Am9 G |
| F5  Fadd9 (F) F5  Fadd9 | F5  Fadd9 (F) F5  G ‖
```

Verse 2
(Female)

```
| A5                 | A5            G |
    Don't throw your - self like that
| F5                 | F5      G |
   In front of me.___
| A5                 | A5            G |
   I kissed your mouth, your back,
| F5                   | Fadd9     |
   Is that all you need?
```

Pre-chorus 2

```
| G                     | Fadd9          |
   Don't drag my love      around, and
| G               | Fadd9
   Volcanoes melt me down.
```

Chorus 2
(both)

```
N.C.        G ‖Am9
And what I     am to you
            |Fmaj7
Is not real,
        G |Am9
What I     am to you,
          G |Fmaj7
You do not need.
        G |Am9
What I     am to you,
        G         |Fmaj7
Is not what you     mean to me,
                     G |Am9
But you give me miles and miles of mountains,
       |Fmaj7
And  I'll ask…
```

Bridge
(Male)

```
                 |C
What I give   to you
                            |E7
Is just what I'm go - ing through,
                |Am
This is no - thing new,
                        |Fmaj7                        |C
No, no, just an  -  other phase I'm finding what I   really need,
           |E7
Is what   makes me bleed,
              |Am                        |Fmaj7                    ‖
But like a   new disease, but Lord she's   still too young to treat.____
```

What I

Outro

|: A5 | A5 |
___ She's still too young, she's still too young,
am to you is not real.___ What I
Vol - ca - noes melt you down.

| F5 | F5 :|
___ She's still too young, she's still too young,
am to you, you do not need.___ What I
Vol - ca - noes melt you down.

|: Am9 | Am9 |
___ She's still too young, she's still too young,
am to you, is not real.___ What I
Vol - ca - noes melt you down.

| Fmaj7 | Fmaj7 :|
___ She's still too young, she's still too young,
am to you you do not need.___ What I
Vol - ca - noes melt you down.

| A5 | A5 |
___ She's still too young, she's still too young,
am to you is not real.___ What I
Vol - ca - noes melt you down.

| F5 | F5 |
___ She's still too young, she's still too young,
am to you, you do not need.___ And what I
Vol - ca - noes melt you down.

| A5 | A5 |
___ She's still too young, she's still too young,
am to you is not real.___ And what I
Vol - ca - noes melt you down.

| F5 | N.C. |
___ She's still too young, she's still too young, you do not
am to you is not real.___ What I
Vol - ca - noes melt you down.

| F5 ||
need me.

WHERE ARE YOU TONIGHT?

Words and Music by Andrew Stewart

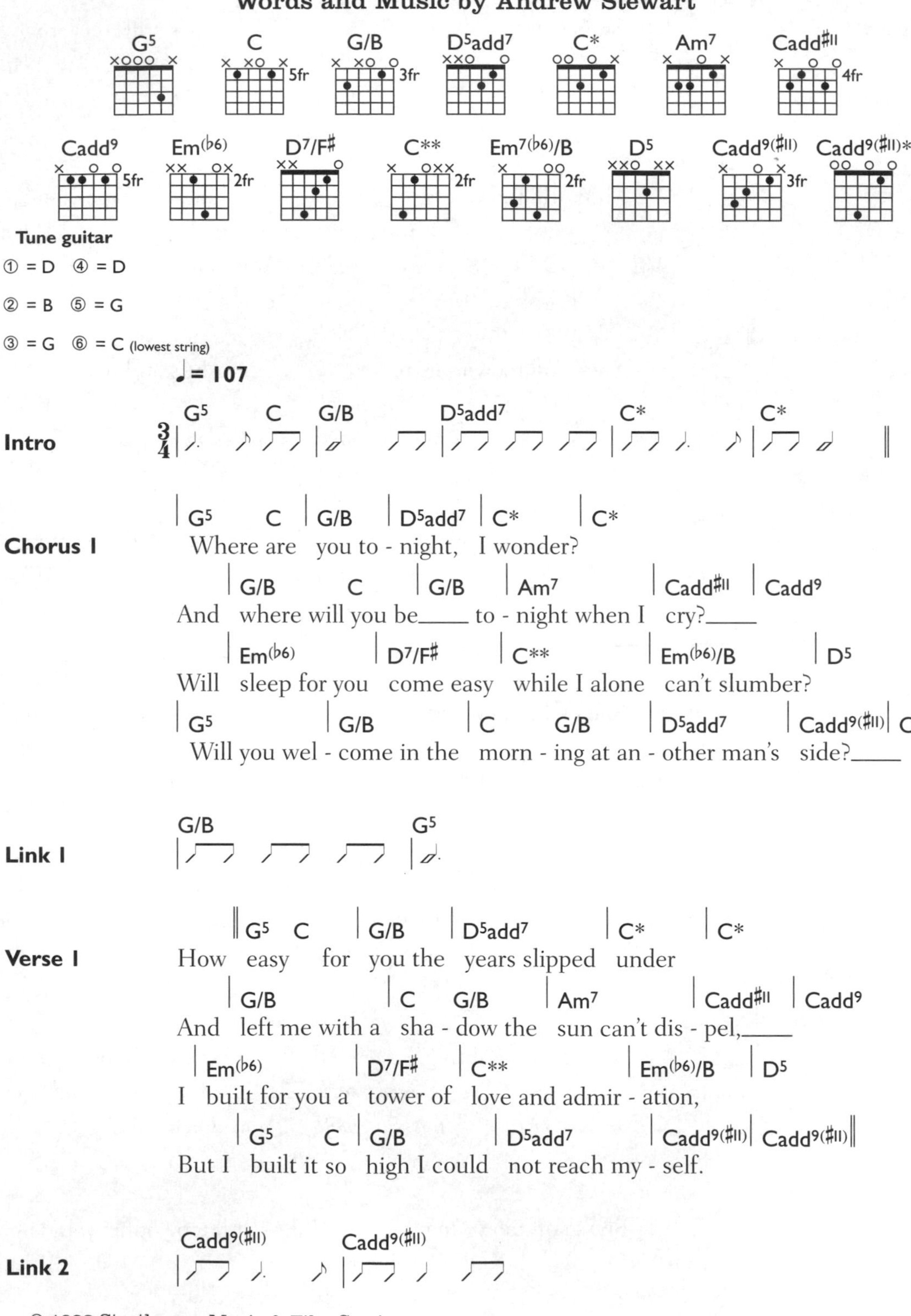
G5 C G/B D5add7 C* Am7 Cadd♯11
Cadd9 Em(♭6) D7/F♯ C** Em7(♭6)/B D5 Cadd9(♯11) Cadd9(♯11)*
5fr 3fr 4fr 2fr 2fr 2fr 3fr
Tune guitar
① = D ④ = D
② = B ⑤ = G
③ = G ⑥ = C (lowest string)
♩= 107
Intro
G5 C G/B D5add7 C* C*
Chorus 1
G5 C G/B D5add7 C* C*
Where are you to - night, I wonder?
G/B C G/B Am7 Cadd♯11 Cadd9
And where will you be to - night when I cry?
Em(♭6) D7/F♯ C** Em(♭6)/B D5
Will sleep for you come easy while I alone can't slumber?
G5 G/B C G/B D5add7 Cadd9(♯11) Cadd9(♯11)
Will you wel - come in the morn - ing at an - other man's side?
Link 1
G/B G5
Verse 1
G5 C G/B D5add7 C* C*
How easy for you the years slipped under
G/B C G/B Am7 Cadd♯11 Cadd9
And left me with a sha - dow the sun can't dis - pel,
Em(♭6) D7/F♯ C** Em(♭6)/B D5
I built for you a tower of love and admir - ation,
G5 C G/B D5add7 Cadd9(♯11) Cadd9(♯11)
But I built it so high I could not reach my - self.
Link 2
Cadd9(♯11) Cadd9(♯11)

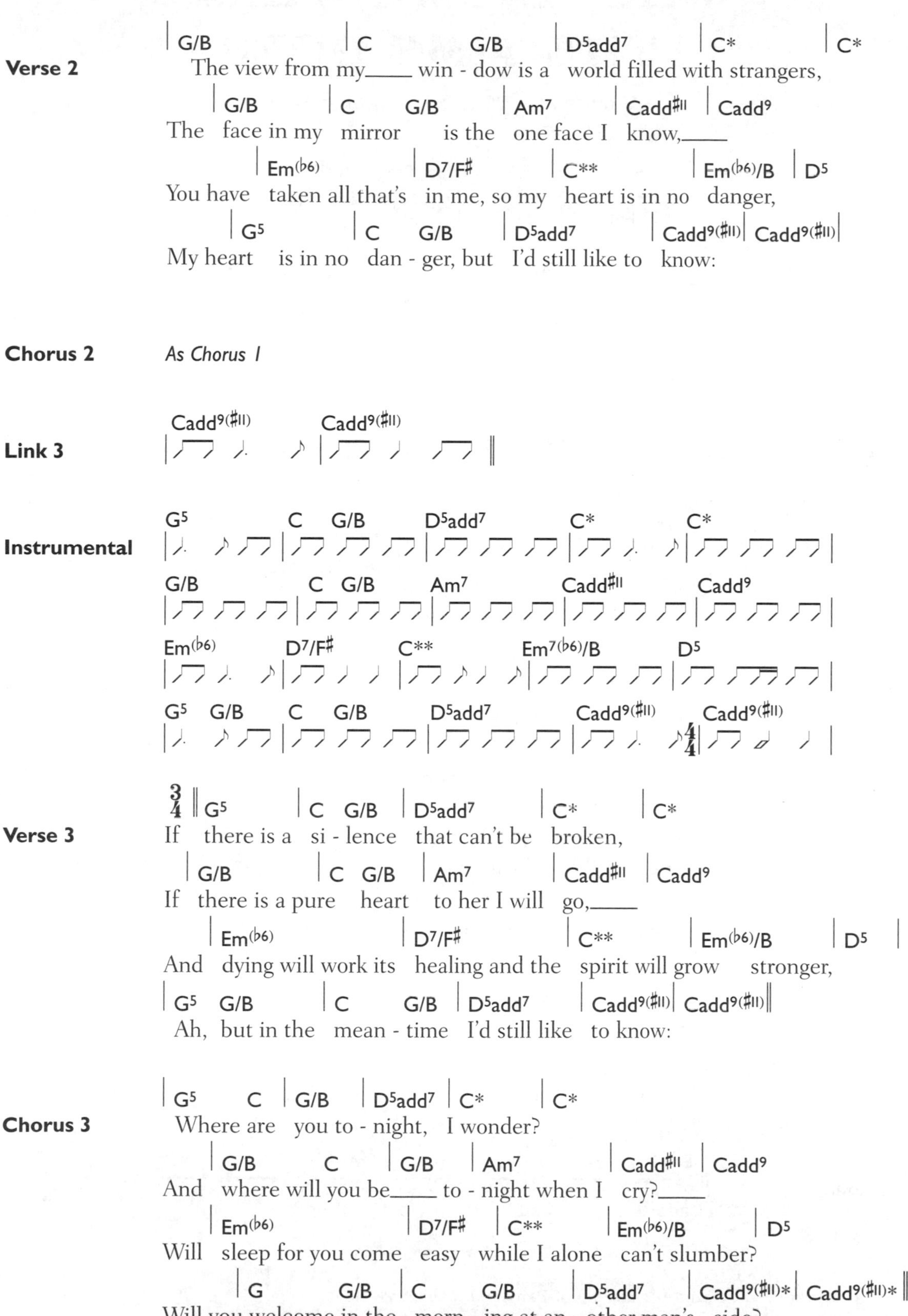
Verse 2
G/B C G/B D5add7 C* C*
The view from my___ win - dow is a world filled with strangers,
G/B C G/B Am7 Cadd#11 Cadd9
The face in my mirror is the one face I know,___
Em(b6) D7/F# C** Em(b6)/B D5
You have taken all that's in me, so my heart is in no danger,
G5 C G/B D5add7 Cadd9(#11) Cadd9(#11)
My heart is in no dan - ger, but I'd still like to know:
Chorus 2
As Chorus 1
Link 3
Cadd9(#11) Cadd9(#11)
Instrumental
G5 C G/B D5add7 C* C*
G/B C G/B Am7 Cadd#11 Cadd9
Em(b6) D7/F# C** Em7(b6)/B D5
G5 G/B C G/B D5add7 Cadd9(#11) Cadd9(#11)
Verse 3
G5 C G/B D5add7 C* C*
If there is a si - lence that can't be broken,
G/B C G/B Am7 Cadd#11 Cadd9
If there is a pure heart to her I will go,___
Em(b6) D7/F# C** Em(b6)/B D5
And dying will work its healing and the spirit will grow stronger,
G5 G/B C G/B D5add7 Cadd9(#11) Cadd9(#11)
Ah, but in the mean - time I'd still like to know:
Chorus 3
G5 C G/B D5add7 C* C*
Where are you to - night, I wonder?
G/B C G/B Am7 Cadd#11 Cadd9
And where will you be___ to - night when I cry?___
Em(b6) D7/F# C** Em(b6)/B D5
Will sleep for you come easy while I alone can't slumber?
G G/B C G/B D5add7 Cadd9(#11)* Cadd9(#11)*
Will you welcome in the morn - ing at an - other man's side?___

WHO KNOWS WHERE THE TIME GOES

Words and Music by Sandy Denny

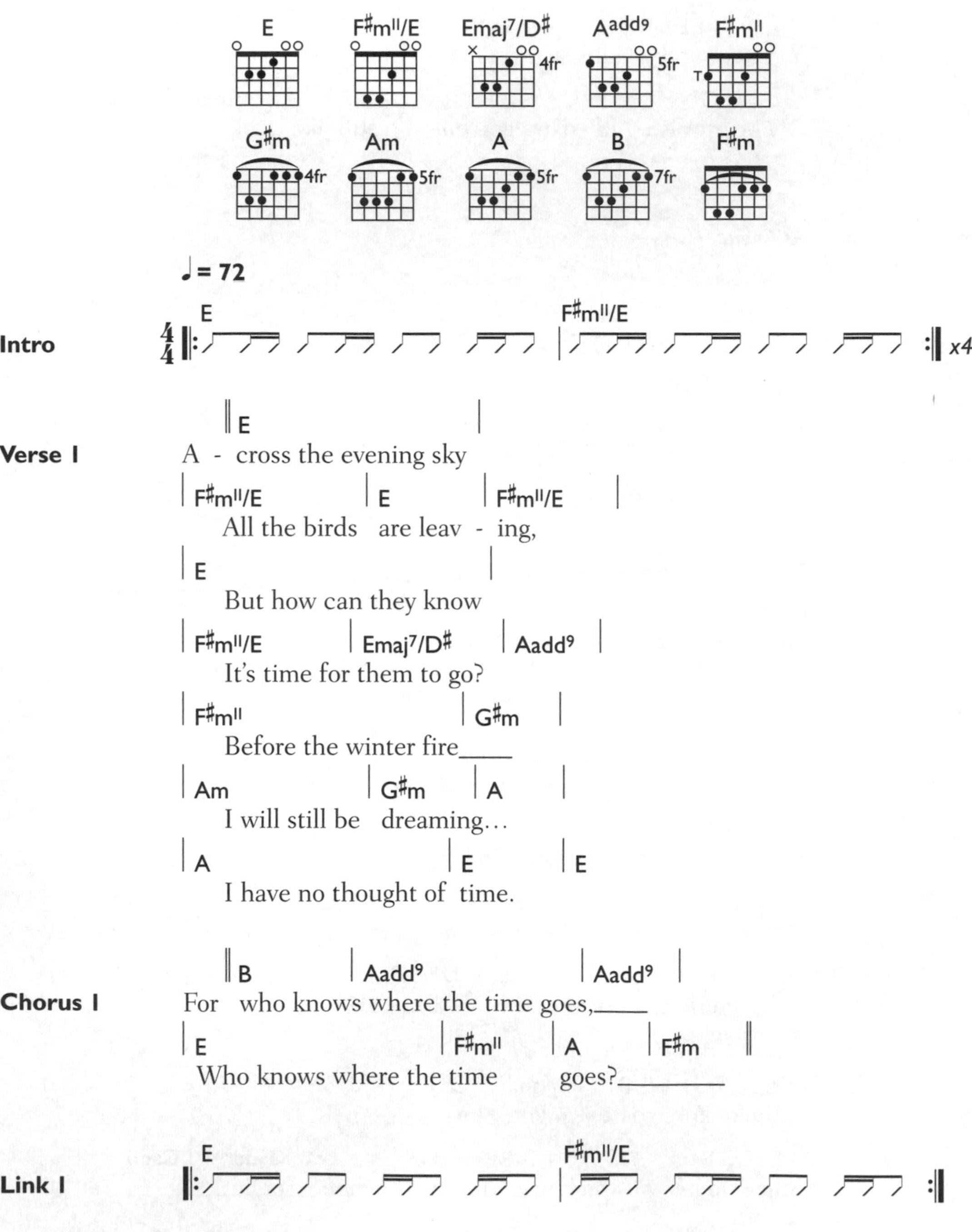

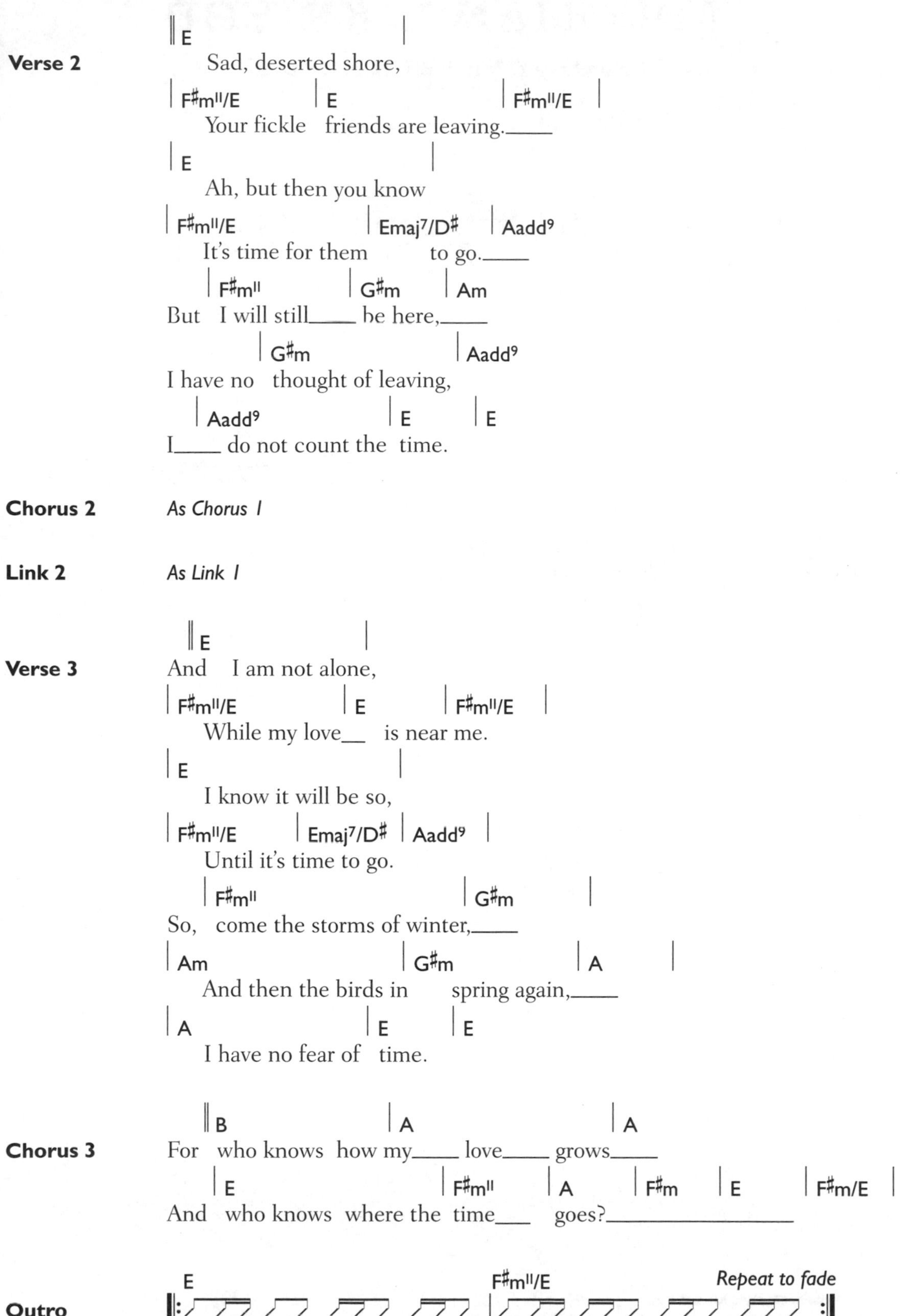
Verse 2
E
Sad, deserted shore,
F#m11/E | E | F#m11/E
Your fickle friends are leaving.
E
Ah, but then you know
F#m11/E | Emaj7/D# | Aadd9
It's time for them to go.
F#m11 | G#m | Am
But I will still be here,
G#m | Aadd9
I have no thought of leaving,
Aadd9 | E | E
I do not count the time.
Chorus 2
As Chorus 1
Link 2
As Link 1
Verse 3
E
And I am not alone,
F#m11/E | E | F#m11/E
While my love is near me.
E
I know it will be so,
F#m11/E | Emaj7/D# | Aadd9
Until it's time to go.
F#m11 | G#m
So, come the storms of winter,
Am | G#m | A
And then the birds in spring again,
A | E | E
I have no fear of time.
Chorus 3
B | A | A
For who knows how my love grows
E | F#m11 | A | F#m | E | F#m/E
And who knows where the time goes?
Outro
E | F#m11/E
Repeat to fade

A WOMAN LIKE YOU

Words and Music by Bert Jansch

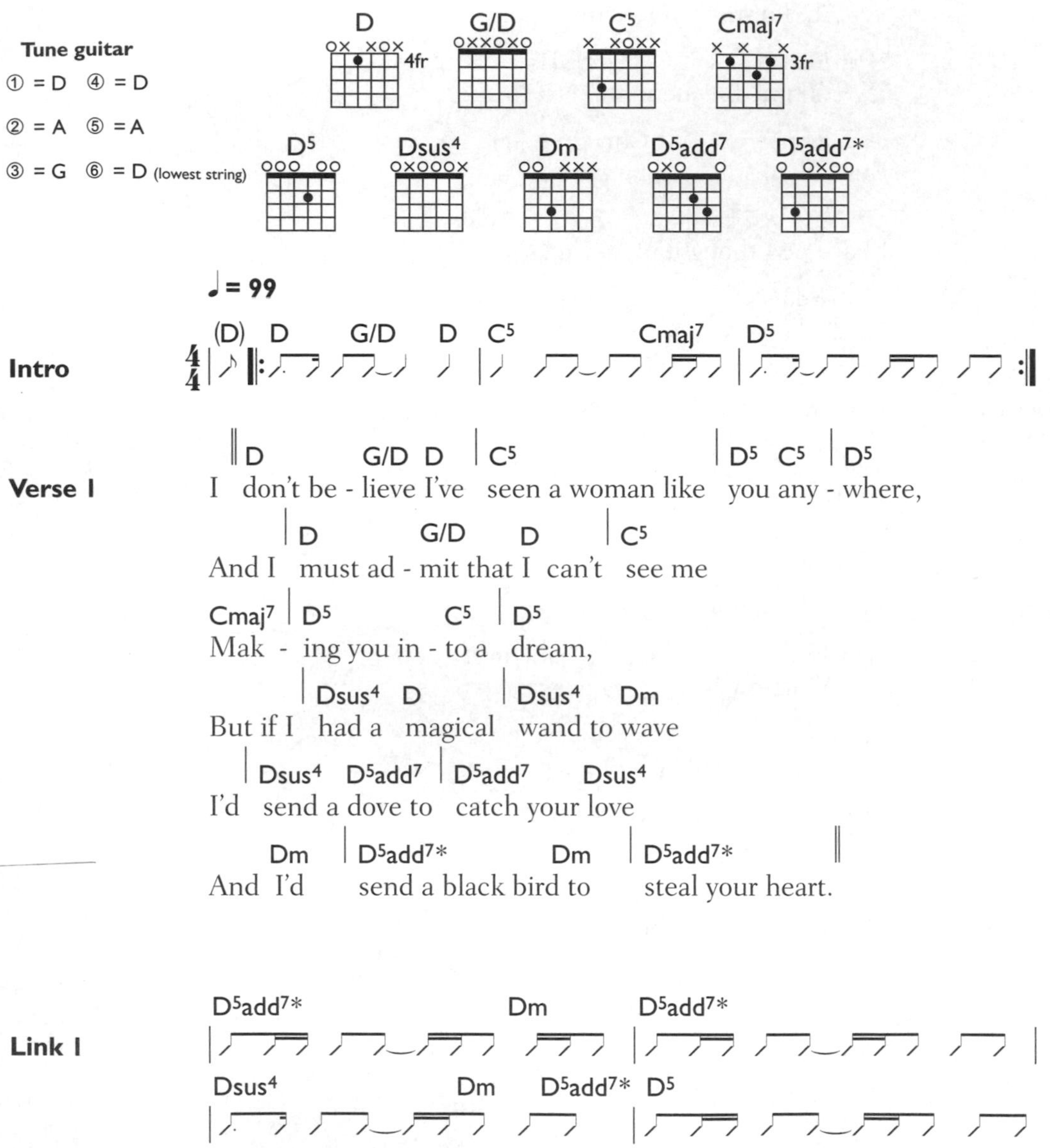

Verse 2

‖ D G/D D | C^5 Cmaj^7 | D^5 C^5 | D^5
But a broken heart won't cure my endless search, little girl.

| D G/D D | C^5 Cmaj^7 | D^5 C^5 | D^5
I'm gonna fix a ma - gical spell to weave on you, little girl.

| Dsus^4 D | Dsus^4 Dm
Of all the long grass to catch you in,

| Dsus^4 D^{5}add^7 | D^{5}add^7 Dsus^4
Of all the orange do sleep in sin?

Dm | D^{5}add^7* Dm | D^{5}add^7* Dm ‖
The Father's glaring round my table here.

Instrumental

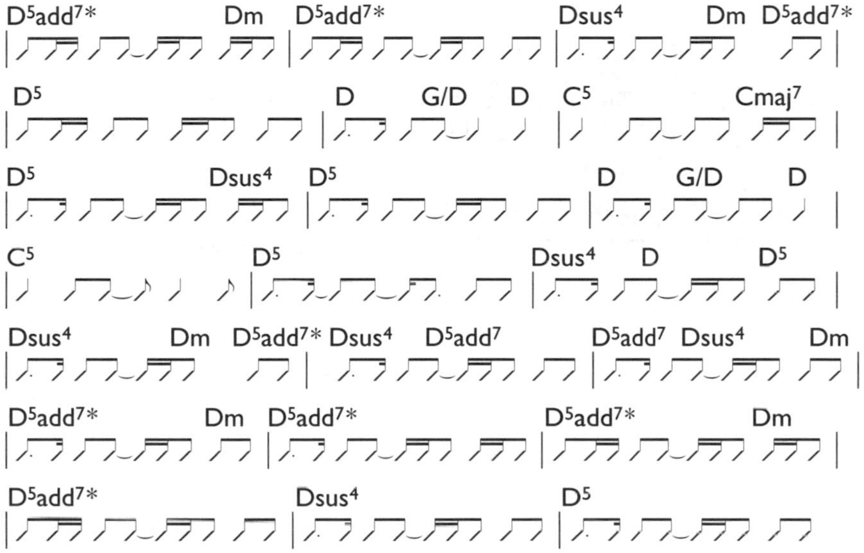

| D^{5}add^7* Dm | D^{5}add^7* | Dsus^4 Dm D^{5}add^7* |

| D^5 | D G/D D | C^5 Cmaj^7 |

| D^5 Dsus^4 | D^5 | D G/D D |

| C^5 | D^5 | Dsus^4 D D^5 |

| Dsus^4 Dm D^{5}add^7* | Dsus^4 D^{5}add^7 | D^{5}add^7 Dsus^4 Dm |

| D^{5}add^7* Dm | D^{5}add^7* | D^{5}add^7* Dm |

| D^{5}add^7* | Dsus^4 | D^5

Verse 3

‖ D G/D D | C^5 | D^5 C^5 | D^5
I'd rather wait and die a thousand times little girl,

| D G/D D | C^5 | D^5 | C^5 D^5
Then take a wo - man in - to my heart__ and my soul.__

| Dsus^4 D | Dsus^4 Dm
And if I caught you sleeping a - long the ways

| Dsus^4 D^{5}add^7 | D^5
I'd carry you off to my secret lair,

| D^{5}add^7* Dm | D^{5}add^7* Dm |
There I'd bind your heart to my very soul.

Link 2

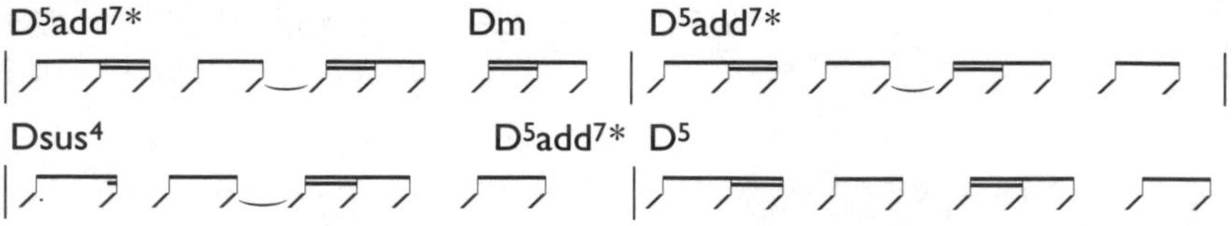

D5add7* Dm D5add7*

| / / / / / / / / / / | / / / / / / / / / |

Dsus4 D5add7* D5

| / / / / / / / / | / / / / / / / / |

Verse 4

```
  || D          G/D  D  | C5                   | D5      C5    D5
I    don't be - lieve I've  seen a woman like   you      any - where,
       | D          G/D       D    | C5      Cmaj7  | D5       C5    D5
And I    must ad - mit that I can't  see me making   you in - to a dream,
           | Dsus4 D       | Dsus2   Dm
And if I     had a magical   wand to wave
   | Dsus4   D5add7  | D5add7    Dsus4
I'd  send a dove to    catch your love
     Dm   | D5add7*         Dm  | D5add7*   Dm  |
And I'd     send a black bird to  steal your heart.
```

Outro

D5add7* Dm

||: / / / / / / / / / / :|| *Repeat riff ad lib. to fade*

Notation and Tablature explained

Understanding chord boxes

Chord boxes show the neck of your guitar as if viewed head on—the vertical lines represent the strings (low E to high E, from left to right), and the horizontal lines represent the frets.

An X above a string means 'don't play this string'.
An O above a string means 'play this open string'.
The black dots show you where to put your fingers.

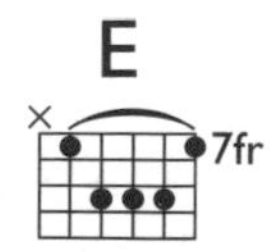

A curved line joining two dots on the fretboard represents a 'barre'. This means that you flatten one of your fingers (usually the first) so that you hold down all the strings between the two dots at the fret marked.

A fret marking at the side of the chord box shows you where chords that are played higher up the neck are located.

Tuning your guitar

The best way to tune your guitar is to use an electronic tuner. Alternatively, you can use relative tuning; this will ensure that your guitar is in tune with itself, but won't guarantee that you will be in tune with the original track (or any other musicians).

How to use relative tuning

Fret the low E string at the 5th fret and pluck; compare this with the sound of the open A string. The two notes should be in tune. If not, adjust the tuning of the A string until the two notes match.

Repeat this process for the other strings according to this diagram:

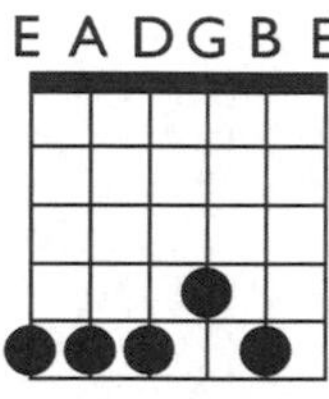

Note that the B string should match the note at the 4th fret of the G string, whereas all the other strings match the note at the 5th fret of the string below.

As a final check, ensure that the bottom E string and top E string are in tune with each other.

Detuning and Capo use

If the song uses an unconventional tuning, it will say so clearly at the top of the music, e.g. '6 = D' (tune string 6 to D) or 'detune guitar down by a semitone'. If a capo is used, it will tell you the fret number to which it must be attached. The standard notation will always be in the key at which the song sounds, but the guitar tab will take tuning changes into account. Just detune/add the capo and follow the fret numbers. The chord symbols will show the sounding chord above and the chord you actually play below in brackets.

Use of figures

In order to make the layout of scores clearer, figures that occur several times in a song will be numbered, e.g. 'Fig. 1', 'Fig. 2', etc.
A dotted line underneath shows the extent of the 'figure'. When a phrase is to be played, it will be marked clearly in the score, along with the instrument that should play it.

Reading Guitar Tab

Guitar tablature illustrates the six strings of the guitar graphically, showing you where you put your fingers for each note or chord. It is always shown with a stave in standard musical notation above it. The guitar tablature stave has six lines, each of them representing a different string. The top line is the high E string, the second line being the B string, and so on. Instead of using note heads, guitar tab uses numbers which show the fret number to be stopped by the left hand. The rhythm is indicated underneath the tab stave. Ex. 1 (below) shows four examples of single notes.

Ex. 2 shows four different chords. The 3rd one (Asus4) should be played as a barre chord at the 5th fret. The 4th chord (C9) is a half, or jazz chord shape. You have to mute the string marked with an 'x' (the A string in this case) with a finger of your fretting hand in order to obtain the correct voicing.

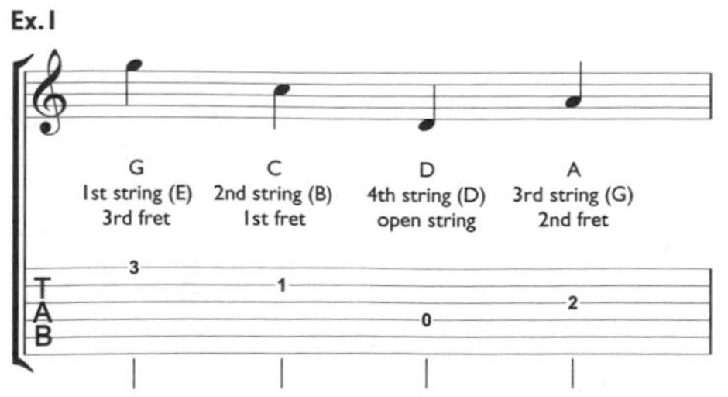

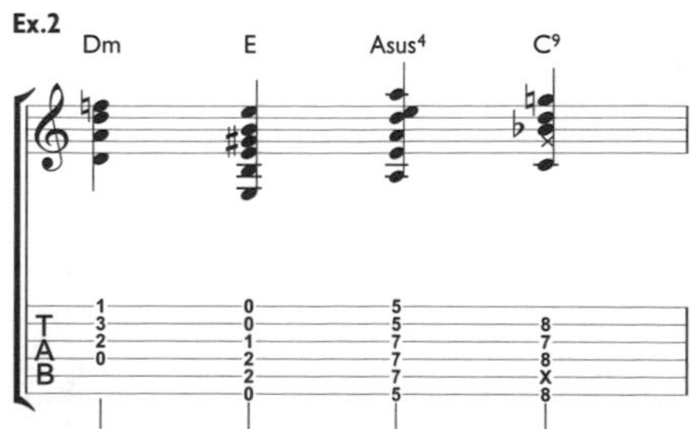

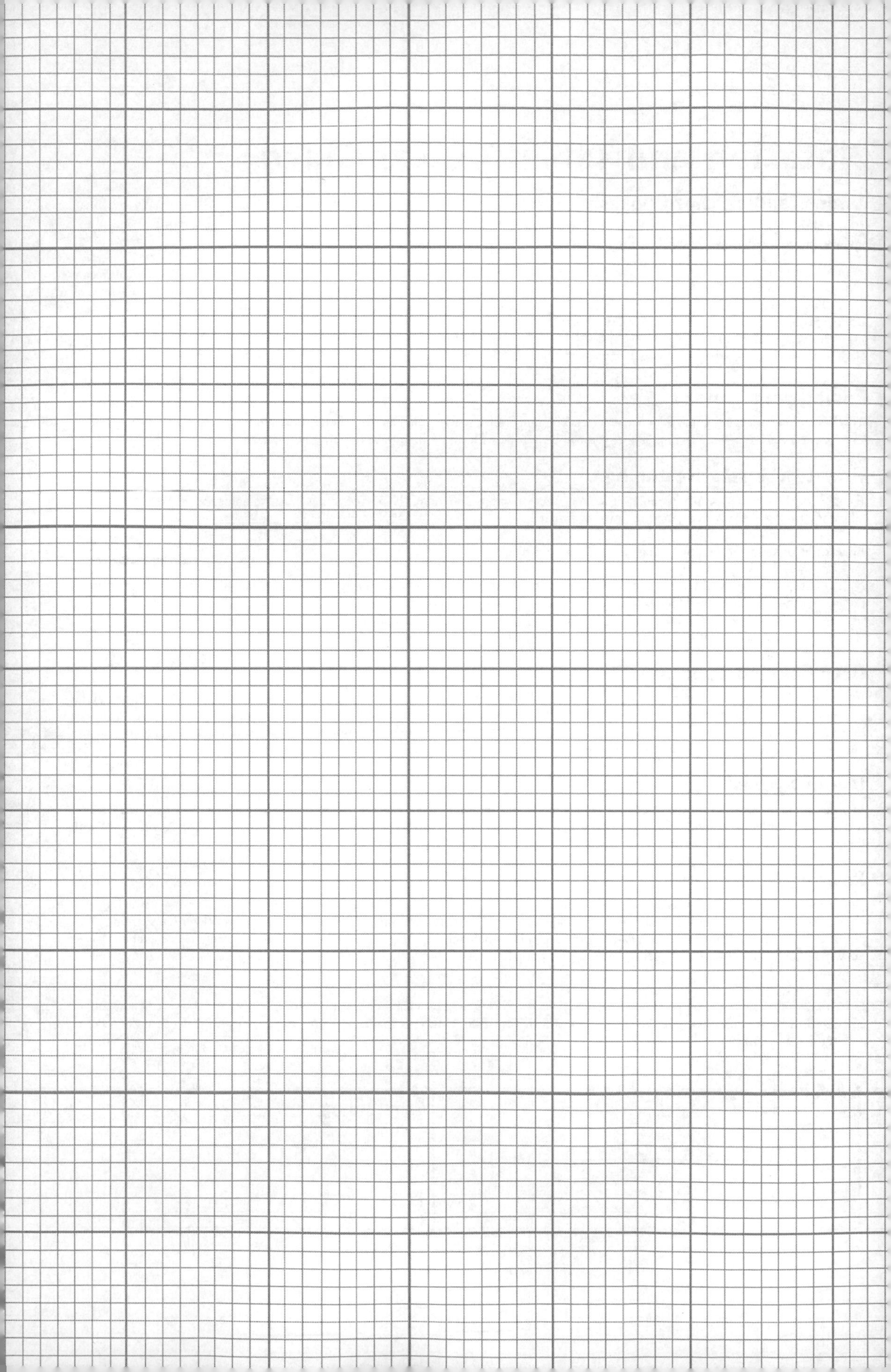

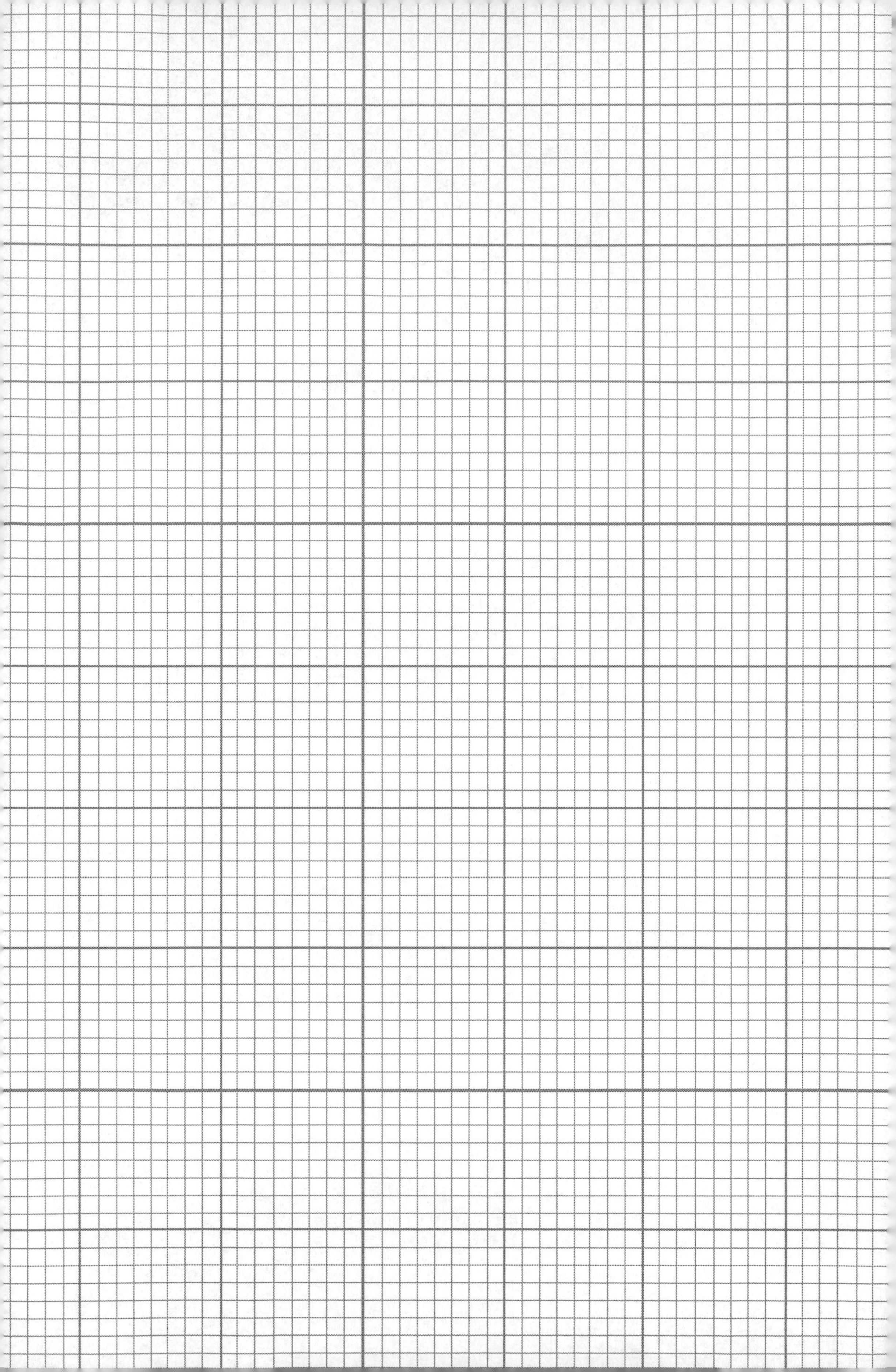

Thirty songs from the most popular contemporary singer songwriters, arranged for acoustic guitar with full lyrics, strumming patterns and chords.

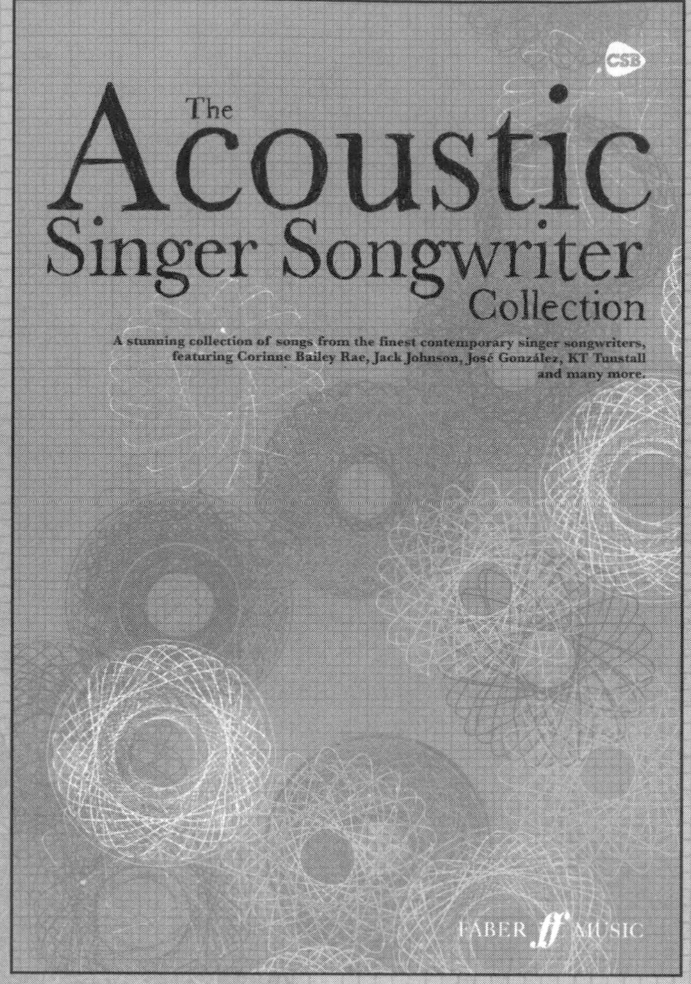
CSB
The Acoustic Singer Songwriter Collection
A stunning collection of songs from the finest contemporary singer songwriters, featuring Corinne Bailey Rae, Jack Johnson, José González, KT Tunstall and many more.
FABER ff MUSIC

Daniel Powter
Jack Johnson
Josh Ritter
Sufjan Stevens
Beth Orton
Damien Rice & Lisa Hannigan
Martha Wainwright
David Gray
Antony & The Johnsons
José González
James Blunt
Jonathan Rice
Morrissey
Nizlopi
Richard Thompson
Jamie Cullum
Kathryn Williams
Ryan Adams
Willy Mason
Corinne Bailey Rae
David Ford
Emiliana Torrini
K T Tunstall
Damien Rice
Rufus Wainwright
Richard Ashcroft
Josh Rouse

FABER ff MUSIC